DON'T HURT A SASQUATCH

And Other *Wacky-but-Real* Laws in the USA & Canada

BY TYLER VENDETTI • ILLUSTRATED BY JUNE LEE

WHALEN
BOOK·WORKS

DEDICATED TO MY FAVORITE NANA, LEX TONELLI.

Don't Hurt a Sasquatch: And Other Wacky-But-Real Laws in the USA & Canada

Copyright © 2021 by Whalen Book Works LLC.

This is an officially licensed book by Whalen Book Works LLC.

13-digit ISBN: 978-1-951511-15-9
10-digit ISBN: 1-951511-15-8

This book may be ordered by mail from the publisher. Please include $5.99 for postage and handling. Please support your local bookseller first!

Books published by Whalen Book Works are available at special discounts when purchased in bulk.

For more information, please email us at info@whalenbookworks.com

Whalen Book Works
68 North Street
Kennebunkport, ME 04046

www.whalenbookworks.com

Cover and interior design by Bryce de Flamand
Typography: Barley, Barley Script, and Brandon Grotesque

Printed in China
1 2 3 4 5 6 7 8 9 0

First Edition

CONTENTS

INTRODUCTION

In September 1620, a merchant ship carrying 102 passengers set sail from a small English town in hopes of finding a better life. After a grueling sixty-six-day journey, these ambitious settlers arrived on the coast of New England. It was here, in the area that we now know as Cape Cod Bay, that the Mayflower Compact was formed. This document laid the groundwork for New England's government and contained some of the first real laws in North America.

A lot has changed since that fateful fall. Once a collection of colonies, the United States is now a fully formed country with over 330 million people spread across fifty states, a handful of territories, and a commonwealth. Its neighbor Canada, with its ten provinces and three territories, has around thirty-eight million. Despite their many differences, both of these countries have something in common: they both live by a series of strange laws that have gone far beyond those of the Mayflower Compact.

Don't Hurt a Sasquatch: And Other Wacky-but-Real Laws in the USA & Canada chronicles those laws, the ones that make us cock our heads and go, "Why does that even exist?" In this book, you'll read about regional laws created by locals for locals, religious blue laws drafted up by puritanical Pilgrims, and laws created simply because somewhere along the way, someone did something stupid and officials wanted to prevent it from happening again.

What you won't find in here, though, are the myths, the ones that have been floating around the internet for years, popping up on sites like DumbLaws.com and driving lawmakers crazy with their absurdity. While some of these outrageous claims are based in (slightly exaggerated) fact, others are rumors started by bored teenagers looking to garner a few laughs or scorned citizens trying to exact revenge on whatever state exiled them. Most of these have no place in this book, unless they've created so much buzz that not correcting them would be morally wrong.

The chapters in this book are broken up by regions and provinces, though how those regions and provinces are defined vary depending on the source you ask. So, if you believe in your heart that you are a Southerner and this book says you are a Westerner, don't panic. The point of these chapters is not to impose an identity on anyone, but simply to highlight how no two corners of North America are alike in their cultures. And that's OK, because at the end of the day, we're all trying to accomplish the same goal: to so thoroughly embarrass our ancestors that they will forever regret leaving Europe to start this freaky continent that we now know and love. So, sit back, relax, and enjoy.

THE MIDWEST

The Corn Capital

Ope! Welcome to the Midwest, where cornfields stretch for miles and no one knows how to say goodbye. Sitting at the top of the country, these twelve states (Ohio, Michigan, Indiana, Illinois, Missouri, Kansas, Iowa, Nebraska, South Dakota, North Dakota, Minnesota, and Wisconsin) have a reputation to uphold as the friendliest corner of the country. That's why, on any given day, you can find them waving frantically at strangers, whipping up cheese curds for the local county fair, and using quaint phrases like "for Pete's sake." When Midwesterners aren't showering you with compliments or inviting you over to their lake house, they are probably cooking up some of their signature dishes like puppy chow, watergate salads, casseroles, and gooey butter cake. So, make sure to arrive with an empty stomach!

ILLINOIS
Cold and Proud

SILLY RABBIT: Once upon a time, you could dye rabbits and chicks and ducklings any color of the rainbow, to the delight of nearby squealing children. But those days have come to an end. Under the municipal code of Chicago, "No person shall bring or cause to have brought into the city, sell, offer for sale, barter or display living baby chicks, ducklings, goslings, or other fowl or rabbits which have been dyed, colored or otherwise treated so as to impart to them an artificial color" (Section 7-12-350). This raises some questions, like what colors are considered "artificial"? Who has the authority to determine that? Is there an artist on the government payroll that makes those calls?

YOU SNOOZE YOU LOSE: You know the saying: there's nothing more boring than cheese. Wait, that's not a saying? Then why does Illinois have a law banning naps in cheese factories? Implemented in 1911, the law states that "it shall be unlawful for any person to sleep, or to allow or permit any person to sleep in any work room of a bake shop, kitchen, dining room, confectionery, creamery, cheese factory, or any place where food is prepared for sale, served or sold." Sleeping on the job is obviously bad, but the specificity of these locations feels strange. Did confectionaries have a problem with bakers using cakes as pillows? Did a creamery worker doze off and drown in a bowl of half-and-half? Did a factory worker collapse into a bucket of melted Gorgonzola? What happened here?

GET OUT THE WAY: If you hate other people, Illinois is the place for you. The city of Galesburg, home of the annual Rubber Ducky Race and Great Cardboard Boat Regatta, has an ordinance on the books forbidding anyone from getting in another person's way. The cantankerous ruling explains that "no person shall jostle or willfully crowd any member of the public in any public or private place, or otherwise interfere intentionally with the peaceful pursuit of their affairs." If any city deserves to have a pair of glaring eyes as their local mascot, it's Galesburg. (To be clear, that's not their mascot. But it certainly should be.)

SQUEAKY CLEAN: The town of Normal, Illinois is anything but. Not only is it the birthplace of Steak 'n Shake and John Winchester (the father of the handsome Winchester boys in the CW's *Supernatural*), but it is also one of the only places in the United States where soap-making is forbidden. Section 21.3-6 of the town of Normal municipal code explains that "whoever shall, within the limits of the Town, establish or maintain any tallow, chandlery, tannery, bone or soap factory, or shall steam, boil or render any tainted lard, tallow, offal or other unwholesome animal substance shall be deemed guilty of a nuisance." In other words, if you're using "unwholesome animal substances" to make your lavender-scented stocking stuffers, or you and your friends are hustling in some dark factory brewing up batches of soap with fanciful names like Holi-Sleigh, then you better watch your backs. Everyone else is fine.

NOAH'S ARK: In the book of Genesis, God announces to Noah that he is going to flood the earth for forty days and forty nights to wipe out all the baddies and assigns to him a very important task: round up two of some types of animals (and seven of others) and stuff them all in a ship so he can ride out the storm and restart civilization when it's all over. Noah agrees and goes on the most chaotic cruise of his life.

While this feel-good tale brings warm fuzzies to most people, to the residents of Colfax, Illinois, it brings great dread. Or at least, we assume so, judging from the strange 2009 Colfax ordinance that forbids its citizens from owning more than two animals of one species. Section 13.24 of the Colfax municipal code states that "it shall be unlawful for any person to own, keep, harbor or possess more than two dogs or more than two cats or more than two of any species of animal in any one dwelling unit or the premises surrounding a dwelling unit." Of course, there's no evidence that any of this has to do with the apocalyptic Bible story, but there's no evidence that it doesn't.

SIT AND SPIT: In the United States, you can risk your life for your country and vote for a president at eighteen years old, but you cannot drink alcohol. But in the state of Illinois, there's one exception. If you are enrolled in culinary school in this Midwestern province, you are allowed to sip whatever alcohol you like, as long as you immediately spit it out. This "sit and spit" bill was approved by the State Executive Committee in 2012 by a margin of twelve to one, and was celebrated by local professors, who argued that young chefs must begin training their palettes much earlier than twenty-one if they're to succeed in the field. In some ways, this makes sense. How are future chefs supposed to know what wine goes best with steak if they don't even know what wine tastes like? How are pilots going to know how to fly if you don't let them up in a plane? How are doctors going to save lives if you won't let them handle a scalpel? It's a slippery slope.

INDIANA

The Covered Bridge Capital of the World

STOP SNIFFING: Kindergartners in Indiana are going to have to find another source of entertainment because glue-sniffing is off the table. In the Hoosier State, "a person who, with intent to cause a condition of intoxication, euphoria, excitement, exhilaration, stupefaction, or dulling of the senses, ingests or inhales the fumes of model glue . . . is guilty of a Class B misdemeanor" (Section 35-46-6-2). Though likely created to stop drug addicts from ingesting glue's intoxicating chemical vapors, the code's explicit inclusion of the word "entertainment" makes it just vague enough to apply to Elmer's-sniffing six-year-olds who are getting a little too curious in their arts and crafts classes.

LET THEM EAT PI: People love pi. Not the food, though people love that too, but the mathematical constant with over 31 trillion digits used to determine the circumference of a circle. This iconic number is revered by math geeks, who have dedicated a whole holiday to the value (March 14 a.k.a. 3.14) and have formed competitions around memorizing the pi sequence (the world record is 100,000 correct digits).

It might surprise you, then, that in 1897, an Indiana physician named Edward Goodwin tried to eliminate pi, claiming that he had discovered a way to find the area of a circle without the use of the complicated number. Though most mathematicians scoffed at his theory, one man, Indiana representative Taylor Record, was intrigued and agreed to Goodwin's plea to draft a bill that would legally change the value of pi from its original value to simply 3.2. Built into the bill was a stipulation that Goodwin would get royalties if anyone in the country used his new pi theory, so he was devastated when, after miraculously passing in the House Education Committee and the house (both unanimously), the bill died in the senate. This is partially thanks to a local university professor named Clarence Waldo, who managed to convince the state's senators that changing a universally accepted mathematical constant to help some physician get a couple of bucks was a bad idea.

HANDS ALONE: In Indiana, if you want to fish, it's the state's way or the highway, and their way exclusively involves fishing poles and bait. According to chapter 9 of the Indiana code, there are many "unlawful means of taking fish" that are unacceptable, including using electric currents, dynamite, poison, and firearms. But the funniest restriction is the one that claims you cannot fish with your "hands alone." Does this mean that fishing with your bare hands is OK as long as you also use your feet? Are fishing with other body parts allowed? Can you crush a fish between your knees without worrying about jail time?

LUKEWARM: Everyone knows that people who drink lukewarm beverages can't be trusted. Why, then, does Indiana have a requirement for liquor stores to sell "uncooled and un-iced charged water, carbonated soda, ginger ale, mineral water, grenadine, and flavoring extracts"? Why would the state enforce these bad habits?

THOUGHTS AND PRAYERS: True to its Midwestern roots, Indiana is committed to its religious traditions and freedoms. It's important to acknowledge, though, when those freedoms go too far, like in the case of Section 35-46-1-5 of the Indiana code, which argues that anyone can legally refuse to pay for their dependent's medical bills and can generally neglect them if they promise to pray on it. Really. The state argues that "it is a defense that the accused person, in the legitimate practice of the person's religious belief, provided treatment by spiritual means through prayer, in lieu of medical care, to the person's dependent child." Let's hope Jesus is listening when Hoosiers ask him to take the wheel at their sick child's bedside.

IOWA

Corny

TOO TAN: Sitting in an artificial tanning bed for hours is not the healthiest activity. While this might be self-explanatory to some, Iowans need a little extra convincing. That's why, if you own a tanning bed in this Midwestern state, you are required to post "a warning sign in a conspicuous location readily visible to persons entering the establishment" that "describe the hazards associated with the use of tanning devices." It's sort of like the pop-up that appears every time you try to avoid purchasing flight insurance: Are you sure you want to do this? Even though it's risky? Even though you could die? Seriously? Fine. It's a free country.

RV VACATIONS: Here's a pro tip: If you're planning a vacation in the state of Iowa, make sure you do it on a Saturday. An antiquated blue law in the state of Iowa prevents residents from buying cars or, more specifically, RVs on Sundays, as part of the religious community's push to reserve Sundays for the godly activities. RV owners across the state have balked at this law, which severely limits the number of weekend days that big, happy families can come in and purchase the mobile home that will inevitably tear them all apart on their next cross-country road trip.

FAKE BUTTER: It's hard to believe that something is really not butter when it looks like butter, tastes like butter, and is advertised using the same exact images as butter. Thankfully, Iowa agrees. They say as much in Section 192.143 of their state code, which demands that any form of imitation butter be called oleomargarine. The law even takes its separation of butter and fake butter further by prohibiting the use of dairy symbolism on imitation butter advertisements. That means no cows, no cream, and no charming milkmen. The people deserve to know what the spread they're slathering on their morning bagel is made from, so they can chomp on their breakfast in peace.

HORSING AROUND: Horses should not eat fire hydrants. Why? Because they're rock-hard, bolted to the ground, and covered in dog pee that has been baking in the sun for God knows how long. It seems pretty self-explanatory, right? Probably, but just to be safe, one town in the Hawkeye State wrote up a code back in 1937 reminding residents not to "fasten, hitch, or tie any horse or other animal to any fire hydrant, telegraph, telephone, electric light or other pole or to any fence, tree, shrub or other property" just in case said animal decides to "bite, eat or in any way damage any fire hydrant, telegraph, telephone, electric light or other pole or any fence, tree, shrub or other property."

SNOW MO: I don't know who needs to hear this, but elk run fast. Like, weirdly fast. A mature male elk (also known as a bull) can gallop up to forty miles per hour on a good day. As a result, hunting them can sometimes be difficult. That's why some Iowans have gotten into the habit of renting snowmobiles for their hunts—machines that can zip through ice and slush at 150 miles per hour like it's nothing.

However, when lawmakers in Iowa caught on to these clever hunting tricks, they decided to put an end to it, adding a clause to their state code prohibiting the use of snowmobiles and aircrafts in the pursuit of big game. The section explains: "a person, either singly or as one of a group of persons, shall not intentionally kill or wound, attempt to kill or wound, or pursue any animal, fowl, or fish from or with an aircraft in flight or from or with any self-propelled vehicles designed for travel on snow or ice which utilize sled type runners, or skis, or an endless belt tread, or wheel or any combination thereof and which are commonly known as snowmobiles." So, spend your money on something a little more worthwhile, like a Tesla or a retirement fund.

BRICK TOSS: Not everyone can grow up in a cool, hip place like New York City or Austin. Some people are stuck in one-stoplight towns, with nothing to do but stargaze, drink, and in the case of Iowa, throw bricks onto highways. Thankfully, there is a "Throwing and Shooting" law that limits such behavior by forbidding anyone (especially teenagers) from throwing "stones, bricks, or missiles of any kind or [shooting] arrows, paintballs, rubber guns, slingshots, air rifles, BB guns, or other danger-ous instruments or toys on or into any street, alley, highway, sidewalk, public way, public ground, or public building, without written consent of the Council." That last bit is important, because if you somehow manage to concoct an event that requires the use of slingshots, arrows, or rubber guns, and get it approved by the local legislature, then you deserve every bit of fun (and chaos) that you have coming to you.

KANSAS
There's No Place Like It

THE MACHINE ATE MY CHIPS: We've all been there. You're pacing in the waiting room of an auto shop while some man named Earl tinkers with your car, and your stomach starts grumbling, so you stomp over to the closest vending machine for a snack. After inserting a dollar into the money slot, you hear the mechanical churning of the metal rings and watch helplessly as your precious bag of chips topples off the shelf and wedges itself against the glass. Rage bubbles in your chest and you grip the sides of the vending machine like an angry bear.

But then, you stop yourself, because you remember that you live in the city of Derby, Kansas, where it is illegal to hit a coin-operated machine. Section 9.12.020 of the city's code of ordinances clearly states that "opening, damaging, or removing . . . any parking meter, coin telephone, vending machine dispensing goods or services, money changer or any other device designated to receive money in the sale, use or enjoyment of property or services, or any part thereof" is illegal.

EEEEK: Speaking of Derby, Kansas, the city has another strangely specific law regarding the improper use of breaks. Part 10.04.200 of the city's code book states that "it is unlawful for any person or persons, while operating a motor vehicle on the streets or highways of the city, to accelerate or speed the vehicle in such a manner or to turn a corner in such a manner as to cause the tires to screech." No one cares how cool it looked in *Fast and Furious*. We don't want to hear your tires slamming against the concrete. It's 9:00 p.m. Go to bed.

SNOW FIGHT: In 2005, Topeka mayor Bill Bunten threw a snowball at a tree . . . and immediately regretted it when he found out that it was actually illegal. On the books since 1981, the measure points out that "it shall be unlawful for any person to throw any stones, snowballs or any other missiles upon or at any vehicle, building, tree or other public or private property, upon or at any other person in any public or private way or place or enclosed or unenclosed ground." Likely created to prevent residents from accidentally hocking chunks of snow into their friends' eyeballs, the law also strips children of a fun winter pastime, leaving them with nothing but ice-skating and igloo-making to keep them entertained.

FOUNTAINS OF RAIN: When it's ninety-seven degrees outside, your AC is broken, and there isn't a speck of shade in sight, the thought of leaping into a public fountain to cool off suddenly becomes a lot more appealing. But in Wichita, Kansas, that's actually not allowed. The ordinance claims that "swimming, bathing or in any manner immersing one's body or any part thereof, or washing, immersing or setting any clothing, wearing apparel or other material of any type, or in any manner throwing, placing or disposing of any matter in any public decorative fountain or pool, except a city employee in the execution of his duties, is prohibited." So, no matter how humid it is or how many shiny pennies you see glistening under the surface of the water, you cannot, under any circumstances, get in.

YOU CAN'T DIE: Quite often, when somebody dies, their acquaintances romanticize their lives, glossing over all of their bad qualities in favor of words like "selfless," "loving," and "filled with potential." While it's tempting to jump up on your soapbox in these moments and tell the world the truth—that so-and-so was actually a big ol' bully—try to contain your cynicism, at least in the state of Kansas. Protesting or picketing someone's funeral, no matter the reason, is illegal. Not to mention, it might get you a punch in the face from someone's mom or brother or overprotective cousin.

MICHIGAN
Have You Played Euchre?

TRAIN TEQUILA: If movies have taught us anything, it's that trains are good for two things: murder mysteries and getting drunk with strangers. Michiganders, however, are going to have to settle for cold-blooded murder if they want to have an exciting train ride in their state. According to Act 68 of Michigan's 1913 legislature, "No person shall publicly drink any intoxicating liquor as a beverage in any railway train or coach, or interurban car, or give, or cause to be given to any other person therein, intoxicating liquor as a beverage." Purchasing alcohol from a train bar is the exception, but public intoxication on a train is still forbidden, so even if you manage to find a spot at the crowded train bar, you'll have to hold your liquor or else risk being tossed off the moving vehicle like some drifter. (That's not the official punishment for breaking this law, but it feels like it should be.)

SHOCKED TO DEATH: This one seems like a given, but, just to be safe, you're not allowed to electrocute your dog to death in Michigan. Yes, even if they chewed up your favorite pair of shoes. No, you can't zap them for peeing on your bed while you're in it. Listen, you can complain all you want, but it's right there on the page: Michigan's Dog Law of 1919 clearly states that "an animal control officer or other person killing a dog or other animal pursuant to the laws of this state shall not use a high-altitude decompression chamber or electrocution for that killing." See? Go get a muzzle or something if you're so concerned.

WE MUST ENDURE: In the season 4 episode of the hit series *That, '70s Show* titled "Hyde Gets the Girl," Kelso and Bob enter a radio contest in the hopes of claiming the grand prize: a brand-new van. To win, all they have to do is keep one hand on the van until all of the other contestants give up. In Point Place, Wisconsin—where the show is set—it's perfectly legal for groups to engage in endurance contests like this one. However, if the group had hopped across the pond to Michigan, such an activity would have been considered illegal under the state's 1935 Endurance Contest Act, which says that it is "unlawful to promote, conduct, or participate in endurance contests" in any capacity. The law was seemingly repealed in 2015.

VIDEO KILLED THE RADIO STAR: When faced with a loud, annoying radio in Detroit, Michigan, there's only one viable solution: turn it off. No smashing it to smithereens. No throwing it out of an open window. No drop kicking it into a nearby lake. Per Section 750.383a of the Michigan state legislature, all of these actions are considered illegal. The law insists that "a person, without lawful authority, shall not willfully cut, break, obstruct, injure, destroy, tamper with or manipulate, deface, or steal any machinery, tools, equipment, telephone line or post, telegraph line or post, telecommunication line, tower, or post, electric line, post, tower or supporting structures, electric wire, insulator, switch, or signal, natural gas pipeline, water pipeline, steam heat pipeline or the valves or other appliances or equipment appertaining to or used in connection with those lines, or any other appliance or component of the electric, telecommunication, or natural gas infrastructure that is the property of a utility." Sometimes, the truth hurts, but we have no choice but to accept it.

PENNIES: In 1890, a well-intentioned mustached man named Eugene Schieffelin hatched a plan to release a collection of European starlings into Central Park in NYC in hopes of creating a haven for these beautiful, iridescent birds. One problem, though: the birds sucked. Tone-deaf and unabashedly loud, these small, shimmering creatures began multiplying and spreading across the United States like a plague. The infestation became so bad that some places decided to put a bounty on the heads of these birds. Michigan, for example, included a law in their 1941 legislature that encouraged its residents to hunt these "nuisance birds" down: "Every person being an inhabitant of this state, who shall kill a starling or a crow in any organized township, village or city in this state shall be entitled to receive a bounty of three cents for each starling thus killed, and ten cents for each crow thus killed." Sorry, Eugene. It was a good thought.

LATE-NIGHT GOLF: If you were planning on arranging a cute latenight date to a putt-putt course, make sure you check your local ordinances before you go: in some places like Detroit, mini-golf facilities are required to close by 1:00 a.m. Why? Teenagers, probably. What else?

MINNESOTA
Lakes on Lakes on Lakes

DOUBLE BINGO: How many games of bingo is too many? That's the question that lawmakers in the state of Minnesota started asking themselves in 2014 when resident Kate Allen stopped by her mother's nursing home in St. Paul only to discover that "the Land of 10,000 Lakes" has a strangely strict policy on the board game. On this fateful trip, she realized that, not only do nursing homes ban outside guests from participating in bingo, but also they refuse to offer bingo more than twice a week. Surprised by this regulation, Allen approached some local politicians and asked them about this rule, to which they responded: huh? Even though the rules have been around since the 1980s, no one, including members of the state's Gambling Control Board, really knows why. So, when Allen asked them to revoke the law, they readily agreed, wiping it from the record a year later.

HERE PIGGY PIG PIG: When you grow bored of the Mall of America, when you've gotten your fill of the Sculpture Garden, when Minnehaha Park no longer piques your interest, where do you turn? Pigs. Specifically, greased pigs. In the mid-1900s, "pig catching"—a game in which people slather up pigs in oils and chase them down for sport—became a surprisingly popular game in this Midwestern state. So popular, in fact, that in 1971, animal rights advocates had to step in and ban such contests, which were often the main attraction at county fairs. Section 343.36 of Minnesota's 1982 statutes clearly states that "no person shall operate, run or participate in a contest, game, or other like activity, in which a pig, greased, oiled or otherwise, is released and wherein the object is the capture of the pig, or in which a chicken or turkey is released or thrown into the air and wherein the object is the capture of the chicken or turkey. Any violation of this section is a misdemeanor." So, if you're looking for a game where you poke and prod at animals, maybe try Pin the Tail on the Donkey instead.

LOVE THAT DIRTY TIRE: There's a scene in every comedy film where a down-on-their-luck protagonist drudging down the sidewalk gets splashed with mud by a passing car, making their dreary day even more depressing. That wouldn't fly in Minnesota. The town of Minnetonka has literally declared muddy tires a nuisance, noting that "a truck or other vehicle whose wheels or tires deposit mud, dirt, sticky substances, litter or other material on any street or highway . . . are nuisances affecting public peace, safety and general welfare."

STATE OF FAIRS: There aren't many things that Minnesota takes more seriously than their state fairs. From giant slides to petting zoos to hay mazes, this local attraction is as much a part of the region's personality as calling soda "pop." That's why the state made a law back in 1933 that forbid any other events from being held around the same time as the fair. Section 37.26 of the 2002 Minnesota code outlines this prohibition in detail: "It is unlawful for any person, firm, or corporation to conduct any circus in any city or within a radius of six miles of any city within a period of eighteen days immediately preceding the dates of the annual Minnesota state fair or during the fair. A circus may be exhibited during this time, however, if and when it is engaged or contracted by an accredited agricultural society to form a part of the entertainment program of the annual fair of the accredited agricultural society."

That's not even the weirdest part. In 2003, the state legislature pushed to eliminate this antiquated law, which most people were excited about. The craziest part? It worked. The bill made it past the house and into the senate and, ultimately, into the hands of the governor, who eagerly signed it. And that's the state of (af)fairs in Minnesota.

BAN THE BUSH: If you've ever been to Minnesota, then you know that they love their wheat. They have museums dedicated to it. Statues erected in its honor. Fields of yellow straw gracing its borders. It's for precisely this reason that they care so much about the barberry bush—a colorful deciduous plant known for brightening up lawns and also destroying wheat on a large scale. Thankfully, Minnesotans figured out the bush's negative qualities—mainly, its association with the plant-based disease stem rust—early on, inspiring them to design an across-the-board ban on this prickly bush around World War I (you know, because a pretty plant wiping out food supplies across the Midwest might not bode well for civilians already suffering from a wartime shortage). A barberry eradication program was formed. Words were exchanged. Bushes were lost. It was all a mess.

THAT AIN'T STRAW: Still not convinced that Minnesota loves its straw? Then how's this: around 1905, the state devised a law stating that "any person not duly appointed and qualified who shall assume to act as a weigher or inspector of hay and straw shall be guilty of a misdemeanor and punished by a fine of not less than fifty nor more than one-hundred dollars." Put another, sillier way: you cannot impersonate a straw inspector in the state of Minnesota. Don't do it. It's no good.

MISSOURI
It's Not Pronounced "Misery"

YARD-SALE HUNTING: Yard sales are the perfect way to knock out two birds with one stone: not only do you get the opportunity to toss out all of the useless knickknacks that you've been holding onto (you won't find a use for that wooden duck statue, I promise), but also you get to make a quick buck while doing it. One town in Missouri went so far as to legally limit the number of yard sales peoople can host in one year. The ordinance states that "no more than two such permits may be issued to one residential premise during any calendar year" and "each garage sale shall be limited to no more than the daylight hours of three consecutive days." The chapter includes other strange restrictions as well, including limits on how long before the sale you can put up signs (twelve hours), protocol for inclement weather interruptions, and rules against "boisterous" behavior on site.

SLEEP ON IT: Let's say you live in Missouri and you get caught transporting a tagless, unlabeled mattress over the state lines. Maybe you were told that Kansas mattresses were better quality and decided to take a road trip to confirm the theory. Maybe you have squirreled away hundreds of dollars within the lining of your mattress and wanted to sneak it out of the state inconspicuously. Maybe labels make your skin itch, and you decided to tear it off. No matter what your reasons were, the punishment is all the same, thanks to one Missouri statute from 2005 that forbids anyone (but particularly mattress sellers) from altering a mattress label or distributing a mattress without one. It might seem silly, but if you think about it, this rule actually makes a lot of sense. Without this law in place, who's to say Mattresses-R-Us wouldn't try to sell you a mattress filled with spiderwebs or marshmallows or some other questionable material?

I CAN'T BELIEVE IT'S NOT BUTTER: Missouri has a long history with farmland, BBQ, and strangely, fake butter. Back in 1895, as butter-alternative products like margarine were on the rise, dairy farmers began scrambling to save their industry. One idea they had was to ban margarine manufacturers from dyeing their product yellow, a color that looked far more appetizing than the spread's natural color: gray. With the help of lawmakers, farmers were able to enact this plan, passing restrictions on imitation butter that helped quell some of their competition. The ruling was in place until 2010, when the state eliminated the bill along with hundreds of other expired and strange provisions.

PURDY FEET: In the 1984 movie *Footloose*, a young Chicago teenager, Ren MacCormack, moves to a Midwestern town only to discover the town has placed a ban on dancing. Upset by this, Ren begins recruiting his peers to dance-offs in hopes of pressuring the town to reverse the ruling. While the film was based on real-life events that occurred in Oklahoma, you'd be surprised to know that this wasn't the only small town implementing such restrictions around this time.

In 1986, in the heart of Missouri, a lawsuit was brewing between the hyper-religious Purdy school district, who believed dancing was a gateway to other sinful activity, and concerned parents, who were upset that their children were driving long distances to attend "unofficial" dances simply because the school did not want to host dances on their property. Two years later, in 1988, after the release of *Footloose* had spurred a larger national conversation about dance bans, a district judge ruled the dancing rule as unconstitutional and reversed it, to the delight of teenagers and Kevin Bacon stans everywhere. But the fun didn't last long. In 1990, the state supreme court handed the schools of Purdy a win by ruling that they could reinstate the dancing ban, which they promptly did.

BACHELOR IN PARADISE: If someone ever tries to tell you that America doesn't discriminate against unmarried people, mention the bachelor tax. Created to reinforce the moral value of marriage, this tax has been implemented in states across the United States for hundreds of years. In Missouri in 1821, unmarried men were taxed a dollar per year (which would be around twenty dollars in today's world) if they had not found a partner. Interestingly, that law is still on the books, but the price has not been adjusted for inflation, leading to every Missouri man between the ages of twenty-one and fifty to be taxed exactly one dollar for every year they go without putting a ring on it.

NEBRASKA
Where Everybody Knows Everybody

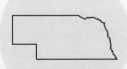

STDON'T: Normally, it's not polite to ask what's going on in someone's pants, but Nebraska lawmakers have a good reason to. According to the Nebraska legislature, "no person who is afflicted with a venereal disease shall marry in this state" (42-102). While it's been on the books since at least 1944, no one really knows how it got there in the first place or whether or not it's regularly enforced. It hasn't even really questioned until 2020, when a Democratic senator, Matt Hansen, finally put his foot down and requested that the law be revised. His reason? A constituent of his had recently demanded an addendum to the rule, one that would allow newlyweds to annul their marriage if they discovered post-ceremony that their partner had an undisclosed STD. Whether or not a referral to a therapist was included in his request is unclear.

LIQUOR THEN BEER, YOU'RE NOT IN THE CLEAR: In Nebraska, you can drink anything. Well, almost anything. The state allows boozy cocktails like Screwdrivers and high-alcohol drinks like Absinthe but there is one beverage that they will not allow: boilermakers. Boilermakers are drinks that blend hard liquor and beer. That means Irish Car Bombs, Beer Sangrias, and Micheladas are off-limits.

Why? Because back in the days of Prohibition, it was illegal to walk around in public in Nebraska with alcoholic beverages. But there was a loophole: bottled, nonalcoholic beer was allowed, leading many to secretly spike their bottled drinks through the cork, creating what's called "needle beer." In response, the Nebraska state legislature had to make a rule forbidding such activity, a rule that has remained on the books all these years later. The rule is hardly enforced and can easily be circumvented (if you order a whiskey and a stout separately, without telling the bartender that you're going to combine them, you're technically not breaking the law), but that hasn't stopped the strange measure from sticking around.

DOUGHNUT HOLE IN MY HEART: Some people call them munchkins. Others call them doughnut holes. Everyone calls them delicious. But only one Nebraska town calls them illegal. The little globs of dough that bakers remove from the center of doughnuts were banned from the town of Leigh, Nebraska, in 1887—not for any nefarious reason, but because they were simply useless. Farmers didn't believe they could profit from these little sugar balls and wrote them off for years. It wasn't until 1997, over one hundred years later, when a DJ strolled into the town to cover the strange law for his show that lawmakers realized they should probably take it off the books, if only to protect the town's reputation. No one wants to be known as "the place that hates delicious treats."

NO HAIR THERE: Many websites have cited this strange law, which states that in Omaha, Nebraska, it's illegal for barbers to shave a man's chest. While there's no evidence of a law banning this specific activity, there's one that is close enough to be cause for confusion. According to Statute 71-202, which defines the act of barbering, it is illegal for anyone who has not attended barber school to partake in "barbering" activities like "shaving or trimming the beard or cutting the hair." If someone claimed to be a barber and shaved a man's chest, they would be lawbreaking, but why anyone would volunteer to touch a strange man's thick body hair is beyond me.

TINY DRUNKS: They say don't drink and drive, but what about drinking and flying? Per a 2012 Nebraska statute, that's not allowed either. Even a minuscule amount of alcohol in your system can disqualify you from flying a plane. Like, a truly small amount. Like, so small you could probably achieve the number from sniffing an alcoholic beverage. Ready to hear it? OK—a person cannot operate a plane if they have "five-hundredths of one percent by weight of alcohol in his or her body." That means if a one-hundred-pound woman had a single drink, she'd likely be disqualified from getting in a plane in Nebraska. So maybe save the celebratory champagne until after you land, OK?

NORTH DAKOTA
The Other Dakota

NOT THAT BIRD: Planning to literally knock out two birds with one stone? You best hope those birds aren't pigeons. In Fargo, North Dakota, the extermination of pigeons is forbidden under Section 11-1002 of the city's code of ordinances. The article states that "no person, firm or corporation shall exterminate pigeons or other harmful wild birds without first having obtained a permit from the Fargo health department and the application for such permit shall be on forms to be provided by the city and the permit shall specify the method of extermination to be utilized." So not only do you need to apply to kill a pigeon, but in your application you also have to specify exactly how you'll commit the murder. Will you lock them in a room with a cat? Throw them out into a snowstorm? Launch them into the sun with a slingshot? Be specific.

LATE-NIGHT LIGHTS: Those who enjoy kicking back and watching lights explode across the sky late into the evening, might want to stay away from North Dakota. Devils Lake, North Dakota, has strict rules on the use of explosives. One such rule forbids anyone from shooting off fireworks past 11:00 p.m. Another bans the use of fireworks before July 1 and after July 5. Yet another says that no one can sell fireworks before June 27 or after July 5. Basically, if you want to be dazzled, do it the week of July 4 or you're out of luck.

MOOSE TAG: Hey! You there! Does that moose belong to you? Yes, the one cowering in the back of the pickup truck. Can you prove it? Where's its tag? Oh, it doesn't have one? Then you might be in hot water, because in the Peace Garden State, transporting a moose without a tag is a punishable offense. Yes, even if they're dead.

STARS AND STRIPES: All across the internet, there are claims that, in North Dakota, it is illegal to hunt with a zebra by your side. While the phrasing of this law is a little misleading, it is technically still true. North Dakota fish and game regulations state that "it is illegal to use any animal except horses or mules as an aid in the hunting or taking of big game." What falls under the category of "any animal except horses"?

Well . . . exactly that. Cats. Dogs. Mules. Monkeys. Orphaned giraffes. And zebras. So, in a roundabout way, using zebras to hunt big game is illegal thanks to their "not-a-horse" status.

I'M ON A HORSE: Speaking of horses, what are they, anyway? Are they considered a mode of transportation? Can we lump them under the same category as planes, trains, and automobiles? If so, are they beholden to the same rules as such vehicles? Some states, like Colorado and Kansas, seem to think so—riding horses while intoxicated in these places can get you a DUI. But when posed this question, North Dakota said "neigh." In 2019, the North Dakota house of representatives floated a bill that would exempt riders of horses from drunk-driving laws. Its success seemed guaranteed—only one representative voted against it—but when the law made it to the senate, it failed by a narrow margin. So close, yet so far.

OHIO
Only We Can Make Fun of Drew Carrey

LET LOOSE: So, your ostrich got out and you didn't tell anybody? That's a major party foul. That's because in Ohio, per a 2005 code, you are legally required to report your escaped animal within one hour of its disappearance if it "presents a risk of serious physical harm to persons or property, or both." There's no use in trying to lie your way out of this one. When residents see an ostrich chasing children in the park, everyone's going to know.

SUNDAYS ARE SAFE: Planning on swiping a chocolate bar from your local convenience store? You might want to wait until Sunday. Strangely, one section of the Ohio revised code states that "no person shall be arrested . . . on Sunday."

In the same breath, the law also prohibits arrests on Independence Day because, true to its name, everyone should be free on the Fourth of July. The law was added to chapter 2331 of the Ohio code in 1999 and was intended to stop people in debt from being seized on protected days. To be clear, this doesn't mean you can commit any crime on Sundays. This isn't The Purge. Drunk driving, treason, and felonies are exempted from this rule.

PASSING GRASS: Watching grass grow doesn't actually take as long as you think. This beloved plant can easily overrun a yard if left unattended, which is exactly what the city of Canton, Ohio, is afraid of. On the books since the late 2000s, the city's "high-grass" law forbids anyone from growing grass taller than eight feet. This is because grass of that size can attract rodents looking for a cozy, private weed forest to raise their families. Repeat violators will get an even harsher sentence, including a fourth-degree misdemeanor charge and a hefty fine. Why repeat violators even exist is hard to say. Pay a teenager to mow the lawn, like everyone else. There are plenty of poor, pimply youths to go around.

THAT'S NOT DIRT: Coal miners work hard. While your average nine-to-five worker's biggest struggle is the 3:00 p.m. slump, the average miner's biggest struggle is a toss-up between access to clean toilets and maybe breathing. The great state of Ohio recognized this flaw and took steps to correct it, implementing a law in 1995 that demands coal mine owners provide "bathing facilities, clothing change rooms, and sanitary toilet facilities in a location at each mine convenient for the use of all mine employees" and that, most importantly, each toilet has "an adequate supply of toilet paper." Dirty butts will not be tolerated in this workplace.

SEE THE RAINBOW: We know it may be tempting to dye your chicks and bunnies around the holidays (who doesn't love pastel-colored bunnies on Easter?), but if you do, the residents of Akron, Ohio, might want to exchange some words with you. Per chapter 92 of their code of ordinances, "no person shall dye or otherwise color any rabbit or baby poultry, including, but not limited to, chicks and ducklings. No person shall sell, offer for sale, expose for sale, raffle or give away any rabbit or baby poultry which has been dyed or otherwise colored." The question remains: Was this law created to protect the animal's well-being or to spare them from embarrassment? A noble choice either way.

SOUTH DAKOTA
Camouflage Weddings Galore

STATIC: In South Dakota, TV time is sacred. It always is in nothing-to-do places like this, where your nearest neighbor is three miles away and the best source of entertainment is a stack of untouched hay bales. But the town of Huron takes their reverence for television a step further with this law that forbids anyone from causing static: "It shall be unlawful for any person, firm or corporation to operate or cause to be operated in the City of Huron any machine, device, apparatus or instrument of any kind whatsoever causing preventable or avoidable interference with television or radio broadcast receiving apparatus between the hours of seven o'clock a.m. and eleven o'clock p.m. of any day" (Section 9.32.010). Who cares that your grandma needs an X-ray? My show is on; find somewhere else to get that checked out, Ruthie.

SAY CHEESE: Cheese, if you're not shoving fistfuls of it into your mouth like it's the last meal you'll ever eat, is quite boring. It's smelly and goopy and sometimes moldy and honestly has nothing to offer besides sustenance, so it's hard to blame the people of South Dakota for not finding it very interesting. Their disinterest has become so severe that the state had to actually enforce a law to regulate it in certain areas. One such law dating back to at least 1920 forbids anyone from falling asleep at a cheese factory. Chapter 242, Section 9 of The Laws Passed at the Seventeenth Session of the Legislature of the State of South Dakota states that "it shall be unlawful for any person to sleep, or to allow or permit any person to sleep in any work room of a bake shop, kitchen, dining room, confectionary, creamery, cheese factory, or any place where food is prepared for sale, served, or sold, unless all foods therein handled are at all times in closed packages." The existence of a similar law in Illinois suggests that the number of workers falling asleep inside cheese factories is more frequent (and therefore more troubling) than previously thought.

YOU LITTLE MINK: When you hear the word mink, you might think of the 2020 news story about the hundreds of coronavirus-infected minks that, thanks to the gas used to kill them, "rose from their graves" in

Denmark and caused many nervous citizens to run for the hills scream-ing about zombie animals, but, frankly, this is an unfair reputation to give to these little guys, because they are so much more than undead virus carriers. Aside from being adorable, minks—the small, ferret-y cousin of otters and weasels—are known for creating medicinal oils that are frequently used in cosmetic and herbal products.

They are also known for being loners, which makes killing them highly discouraged. In South Dakota, where these animals run wild, there are even laws designed to prevent just that. One law forbids any-one from building a mink den for the purpose of catching and killing the creatures. Section 41-8-24 of the 2006 South Dakota code demands that "no person shall hunt any mink or muskrat with the aid of any dog, or dig, disturb, or molest any mink den or beaver house for the purpose of capturing any of these animals, or use poison, gas, or smokers of any kind to kill, take, or capture any of these animals." In short, the minks aren't bothering anyone. Leave them alone.

SISSETON STAR: Self-defense is important. Buy some pepper spray. Learn karate. Clutch your keys between your fingers like Wolverine. Do whatever it takes to help you feel safe. Just don't, for the love of God, carry around ninja stars. If you do, and you live in Sisseton, South Dakota, you will be handed a misdemeanor and thirty days in jail. The star will also be destroyed because apparently, these sharp, pointy weapons "are not toys" and can be "dangerous" and cause "bodily harm" or "death."

BOOM BOOM: Whatever happened to the good ol' days, when farmers used shoddy, dilapidated scarecrows to guard their crops? Did birds wise up and realize that they were being fooled? Is that why farmers in South Dakota started using fireworks to protect their land? Who knows. Regardless, the practice of using explosives to keep away pesky crop offenders in South Dakota has become so common in recent years that lawmakers had to implement a rule forbidding the practice. What's strange, though, is that the measure doesn't apply to all crops: just sunflowers. Section 34-37-20 of the South Dakota codified laws literally states that the "use of explosives or fireworks for protection of sunflower crops" is forbidden. Any other flower? Light it up. But sunflowers? Forget about it.

WISCONSIN
Ya Know?

HERE COMES THE CHOO-CHOO TRAIN: When you hear the word "Wisconsin," you might think of cheese curds, funny accents, and frigid temperatures, but what you really should be thinking about is trains, because there are a handful of strange laws in place related to these automotives. For example: it is illegal to throw rocks at trains in the Badger State. Per Section 943.07 of the 2012 Wisconsin statutes, "whoever intentionally throws, shoots or propels any stone, brick or other missile at any railroad train, car, caboose or engine is guilty of a Class B misdemeanor." Additionally, it's illegal to throw trash on the tracks or shoot a firearm at any portion of the railcar, so leave those cowboy dreams behind you.

CHIP ME: Someone in Wisconsin has been watching too many science fiction movies, and that someone is State representative Marlin Schneider, a Wisconsin Democrat, who, in 2005, introduced Assembly Bill 290, which forbids anyone from forcefully implanting a microchip in another person's body. Originally made to prevent companies from tracking their employees' every move, the law has some unfortunate unintended consequences. For example, the microchips in question, called RFID implants, have helpful uses outside of tracking Gerald from Finance's location. (Were you just out for a smoke, Gerald, because Find My Workers says that you were hanging out at our competitor!?) These devices can also be installed in Alzheimer's patients and sexual predators to help keep track of their whereabouts, for their own safety and the safety of those around them.

But despite this, Schneider was not deterred in his crusade, claiming that such people deserve the same civil liberties as ordinary citizens. On paper, this makes sense, but in practice, it gets a bit tricky. Just wait until your grandma disappears from the nursing home and you have to go hunting for her. Just wait.

CHEESE PLEASE: Nicknamed America's Dairyland, Wisconsin is the cheese capital of the United States. It all started in the nineteenth century, when European immigrants uncovered the area's vast fertile fields and decided to take advantage of it, establishing dairy farms all across the state. Suddenly, they were up to their eyeballs in milk and needed something to do with all the excess liquid. So? They turned to cheese, constructing upwards of 1,500 cheese factories over the next century. To this day, these cheeseheads are the largest producer of this dairy product in the United States, boasting six hundred different cheese varieties.

Why is this important? Because Wisconsinites are so confident in their cheese-making abilities, they're willing to literally criminalize the production of subpar cheese. Under Section ATCP 81.40 of the Wisconsin state legislature, "the flavor of Wisconsin certified premium grade AA cheddar, granular and washed curd cheese shall be fine, highly pleasing and free from undesirable flavors and odors." The chapter also goes on to outline the texture, color, and "finish" required for a cheese to be considered good. These people are not messing around.

PRISON COOKIES: What Martha Stewart doesn't know might actually hurt her. While America's culinary sweetheart was arrested in 2004 for insider trading, there's another law that the homemaker would be in danger of breaking, if she lived in Wisconsin. Up until 2017, Wisconsin was one of two states in the United States that banned the sale of homemade goods. That means anyone who dared whip up some cookies for a bake sale could land thousands of dollars in fines and potential jail time. It wasn't until the late 2010s, when the Institute for Justice decided to challenge the law in court, that it was ultimately ruled unconstitutional. There are still some important rules in place, though, to ensure this dangerous practice is kept in check. Bakers must follow strict moisture rules to avoid selling undercooked or potentially hazardous goods. Yes, moisture rules. That's what they're called. No one's happy about it.

BUTTER FINGERS: In Wisconsin, it's butter or bust. This dairy-loving state has made it illegal to serve butter substitutes in restaurants (Wisconsin legislature, Section 97.18). That means you can't slap a brick of margarine on the table next to a basket of bread and let those poor, unassuming customers believe they're about to eat smooth, creamy butter. It's deceptive, it erodes the public's trust in Wisconsin's butter quality, and, worst of all, it deprives the state's citizens of a delicious spread that will clog their arteries and shorten their life span. If the people want butter, that's their God-given right, and no one is going to take it away.

THE NORTHEAST
Winter, Winter, Still Winter

Known for its beautiful fall foliage, gnarly accents, never-ending snow-storms, and collective obsession with Dunkin' Donuts, the Northeast is a beloved region of the country composed of nine states: Maine, New Hampshire, Vermont, Massachusetts, New York, Rhode Island, Connecticut, New Jersey, and Pennsylvania. Cherished for its rich sports culture and quaint college towns, the area is also famous for another, notable reason: its history. Back in 1620, Pilgrims fleeing religious persecution in England stumbled upon this sliver of land off the East Coast. Hoping to honor the religious freedom that they'd crossed an ocean for, residents of these states began enacting laws to ensure that Sundays were protected as the Lord's day. These were the original "blue laws," making New England the birthplace of this American trend and adding another historical accomplishment that they can add to their long resume.

CONNECTICUT
The Nutty Nutmeggers

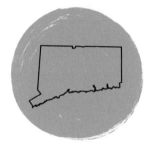

NO ALCOHOL ON SUNDAYS: The state of Connecticut forbids the sale of alcohol on Sundays. At least, they did until 2012 when the governor, Dannel P. Malloy, reversed the centuries-old law. This was kind of a big deal, as the measure had been in place since the 1650s. It had been established by a man named Roger Ludlow, who wanted to give the colony's laws a face-lift. Borrowing ideas from the neighboring state of Massachusetts, he put forward a list of provisions known as the First Connecticut Code. A few years later in 1655, two other members of the community, Theophilus Eaton and Reverend John Cotton of New Haven, Connecticut, made some revisions and broadcasted them to the community, sending out five hundred printed copies of the new rules to ensure the city's compliance. If they only knew that, almost four hundred years later, some man named Dan would throw all their hard work out the window so that his citizens could buy beer for Sunday football games . . .

HAT HAIR: Are you a boy with dreams of growing your hair out like Jason Mamoa or Jesus? Well, if you live in Connecticut, don't bother. Males are required to cut their hair in a mushroom shape to accommodate caps or hats. Can't find a hat to put the haircut to the test? No problem! The hard shell of a pumpkin will suffice and can be used as a guide.

This, of course, isn't entirely true. Back in 1781, Connecticut resident Samuel Peters was banished from New England and forced to move back to the United Kingdom indefinitely. Petty and scorned, Peters decided to publish a semi-historical account of his old colony, complete with a list of absurd blue laws that painted Americans as fanatical religious kooks. To this day, historians are unsure which of the laws enclosed in his book (including this hat hair measure) were real and which were invented to make his fellow Americans look like nutjobs as punishment for exiling him.

SILLY STRING: In October of 1995, two cops riding in the Southington, Connecticut, Apple Harvest Festival parade were struck down by a group of pranksters spraying silly string at their faces. But that wasn't all. Nearby, band members scrambled to wipe the goopy slivers off of their instruments and cheerleaders screeched at the little green lines now staining their turtlenecks. Young marchers in the band—friends of the supposed hooligans—were so embarrassed by the debauchery that they swore off all future parades. The town's attorney decided enough was enough and put forward an ordinance banning the use of silly string in public places. The law passed with flying colors.

THAT'S A PICKLE: Did you know a pickle can technically only be considered a pickle in Connecticut if it bounces? Apparently, in 1948, two men named Sidney Sparer and Moses Dexler were arrested for selling pickles that were considered "unfit for human consumption." The Connecticut food and drug commissioner at the time, Frederick Holcomb, told reporters that in order to check for pickle viability, one should "drop it one foot," and if it bounces, it's safe. To demonstrate, they tested the pickles in question, which kerplunked on the floor, leaving Sparer and Dexler with a five-hundred-dollar fine. While their pickle may have been swiftly destroyed after the incident, a statue that led to it was not and supposedly remains on the record.

DRUNK HISTORY: Think about the guy at your local bar that slumps over the counter mumbling stories about secret government organizations and slurring accusations against his exes into his cognac. Would you want that man in charge of any important documents? No, you wouldn't. Thankfully, Connecticut had the same thought. In 1949, they enacted a rule stating that it was illegal to store town or probate records in any location where liquor was sold. The point of this bill, we assume, was to keep the area's history out of the hands of sloppy drunks who may have wandered into the back room of whatever bar they were imbibing in and accidentally destroyed historical documents. The law was repealed in 2002, for reasons unknown.

MAINE

The Home of Your Grandparents' Beach House

SUNDAYS AREN'T FOR HUNTING: According to title 12 of the Maine state legislature, it is illegal to "hunt wild animals or wild birds on Sundays." While eleven states have some sort of restriction on chasing down bunnies on the Sabbath, only two—Maine and its M-neighbor Massachusetts—have outright bans. This blue law stems from the area's religious history and the community's belief that Sundays should be reserved for praying, churchgoing, and football watching. Local hunters argue that the activity generates money for the state by encouraging the purchase of hunting gear and licenses, but unfortunately for them, the state refuses to budge on the rule, to the delight of deer everywhere.

CAR SALES: Let's say it's a Sunday afternoon and, dismayed by the restrictions on hunting, you decide to engage in your other favorite activity: buying cars. Well, that's too bad: Maine also forbids "the business of buying, selling, exchanging, dealing or trading in new or used motor vehicles" on the Sabbath, per title 17, chapter 105 § 3203 of the Maine revised statutes. Despite the fact that Maine is, as of the early 2010s, considered one of the least religious states in the country, the antiquated blue law still stands, putting a halt to all the teenagers begging their parents for a used Toyota every weekend.

LOBSTER FISHING: Get your grubby hands off Maine's trademark red crustaceans. In this seaside state, "a person may not fish for or take lobster by any method other than conventional lobster traps" (Maine revised statutes—title 12, chapter 619 § 6432). While the explanation for this law likely lies in the state's reverence for its sea life—as evidenced by the shell decor in every local beach house—it's entirely possible that some brave fisherman lost a finger trying to snatch this creature with his bare hands, forcing this rule to become necessary. Other "lobstah" laws include: it is unlawful to possess a pregnant lobster, a mutilated lobster, or an "over or undersized" lobster.
NO SELLING TO THE

DEAD: In some Maine towns, including Dexter, it is illegal to "use any form of advertising on cemetery premises" (town of Dexter, Maine, ordinances—chapter 3.6, , Section 3.6-4). Which means all of those posters you made for Ghost Gowns and Coffin Disco Lights are going to go to waste.

SIDEWALK STUNT: In the town of Farmington, Maine, "no person shall operate, or cause to be operated, any roller skates, skateboard, or scooter upon any sidewalks or streets of the municipality of Farmington in a reckless or hazardous fashion" (Farmington town ordinances—chapter 16). In other words: those rollerblades you got for Christmas? Throw them in your trunk and drive to the next town over, because in Farmington, they're considered dangerous and subject to penalties ranging from a one-hundred-dollar fine to a strongly worded message along the lines of "You could've killed me, Darryl!!"

DUNKIN' DON'T: There is a small town on the tip of Maine that forbids residents from parking in front of the local Dunkin' Donuts. As stated by article III of the town's general legislature, no one can park "in front of [the] Dunkin' Donuts to a point 25 feet south." This is mostly due to the fact this particular Dunks has no designated parking spaces up front, causing many caffeine-crazed customers to lurch into a small alley in front of the store and leave their cars idling as they dash in to grab the goods. This routine has resulted in so many dented bumpers and enraged drivers that the town literally had to make a rule preventing it. Do Northeasterners actually abide by this rule? Considering the abundance of Massholes and road-rage enthusiasts on the East Coast, you can probably guess the answer.

MASSACHUSETTS
It's a Fenway Kind of Day

SPORTS DAY RAGE: You're at Fenway, watching the Red Sox destroy the Yankees, and you see the umpire make a bad call. Rage flares inside you, but before you stand up to give him a piece of your mind, you remember: that's illegal. The 191st general court of the Commonwealth of Massachusetts states in chapter 272 that "whoever, having arrived at the age of sixteen years, directs any profane, obscene or impure language or slanderous statement at a participant or an official in a sporting event, shall be punished by a fine of not more than fifty dollars." Surprisingly, as of 2020, this law is still in place, so if you're planning on getting feisty at your next sporting event, remember to bring your teenager so you don't get fined.

PIGEON PRESERVATION: There are a few things that Massachusetts takes seriously: St. Patrick's Day, Ben Affleck movies, and pigeons. This law relates to that last one. Under the crimes and punishments section of Massachusetts law, it is prohibited to willfully kill or frighten pigeons from beds or nets that have been constructed for the purpose of capturing them. Created in 1848, the law (which is currently still on the books) also states that anyone who disobeys may be subject to up to thirty days in jail and must compensate the person who intended to capture the pigeon for any damages. While this might seem crazy now—pigeons are so prevalent in our society, they're practically considered citizens—back in the 1800s, they were a common food source, making the rules around scaring off someone else's pigeon target quite reasonable. Thankfully, in the years since, most of the world has transitioned to consuming other feathery animals (sorry, chickens), making this pigeon preservation law feel antiquated and downright goofy.

SING IT LOUD: According to one Massachusetts law, some of your favorite Super Bowl performers probably belong in jail. Chapter 264, Section 9 of the Massachusetts general court legislature states that "whoever plays, sings or renders the 'Star Spangled Banner' in any public place, theater, motion picture hall, restaurant or café . . . other than as a whole and separate composition or number, without embellishment or addition in the way of national or other melodies . . . shall be punished by a fine of not more than one hundred dollars." Which is to say, anyone who mangles the US national anthem will not only be held personally responsible by patriotic listeners (probably in the form of a tomato to the face) but also will be held legally responsible by state officials. This is America we're talking about, not *American Idol*.

While it's unclear what prompted this law, one of its most notable mentions describes a Russian composer named Igor Stravinsky who lived in Boston, Massachusetts, during the 1940s. In 1944, he was asked to conduct the Boston Symphony Orchestra and, thrilled at the opportunity to instill a sense of patriotism back into a country ravaged by the Depression, decided to invent his own special arrangement of the "Star-Spangled Banner," adding in a seventh chord and some additional flairs. In response, the Boston police cited this obscure law and demanded that Stravinsky remove the performance from the bill, which he did, reluctantly.

NO BEER HERE: In a state where drunken debauchery is a rite of passage and young men clinging to their Irish heritage roam the streets, it's no surprise that alcohol is considered a problematic substance. What is a surprise is that these concerns extend all the way to the hospital, where medical staff are legally forbidden to give alcohol or drugs to patients who are in the hospital for alcohol or drugs. This rule may seem straightforward, yes, but try explaining it that to the college students that stumbles through the doors of the ER and demands a Sam Adams while being treated for alcohol poisoning.

WHO HELPED THE DOGS OUT: If you are a medical technician in the state of Massachusetts, you cannot help an animal while on the job. So next time you pull up to the scene of an emergency and notice a cat screeching from the tip of a nearby tree? Ignore it. Next time you are doing CPR and catch a dog nursing his injured paw nearby? Look away. Next time you spot a baby bird toppling from its nest while you're resuscitating a drowned child? Pretend it never happened. Under existing Massachusetts laws, medical personnel are forbidden from assisting animals while in the line of duty. While this was originally created to prioritize the needs of human victims, it has resulted in a number of traumatizing stories about injured K9s being left behind in favor of catching the bad guy. This, of course, makes sense, but it doesn't make it any easier to tell Fido that he'll have to wait to have his broken paw looked at. He'll look at you with those puppy dog eyes, and you'll wish you lived in another state.

CERTIFIED NUTJOB: So, you want to buy a house, but your credit score is in the toilet and the bank won't give you a loan. What do you do? In any other state, you might be able to use trickery to swindle someone out of their property, but not in Massachusetts. In the crimes against property section of the state legislature, it says that "whoever, by a game, device, sleight of hand, pretended fortune telling or by any trick, ... fraudulently obtains from another person property of any description shall be punished." Laws such as this are common in the United States and are often referred to as "larceny by trick" crimes, which invalidate any contract made through deceit or fraud, but the language in this Massachusetts code (mainly, "pretended fortune telling") does suggest some deeper history, perhaps relating to sneaky witches who wanted to acquire some property in Salem and decided to take matters into their own scheming hands.

YOU'RE A TRAITOR: Communists, beware. According to chapter 264, Section 17 of Massachusetts general laws, any group considered to be "subversive" is considered unlawful. Why? Because back in the 1940s and '50s, a US senator from Wisconsin named Joseph McCarthy asserted one afternoon that he had a list of people who were known to be affiliated with the Communist Party and he was going to expose them all. This announcement, coupled with rising tensions with Russia, sparked a wave of fear and uncertainty in the country known as the Red Scare. Left and right, people began accusing their neighbors of being communists or working against the government. It even triggered a wave of UFO movies portraying "body-snatching" creatures who were disguised as humans living among us. Following this explosion of Communism-phobia came this law, passed around 1951, that made being a part of such "subversive" groups illegal. It remains on the books to this day.

NEW HAMPSHIRE
Live Weird or Die

KID CEMETERY: In the town of Amherst, New Hampshire, children under the age of fifteen are not allowed to enter a cemetery unless accompanied by an adult. Established in accordance with New Hampshire RSA 289 Cemeteries/Burials, the law prohibits preteens from wandering through cemeteries, drunkenly disturbing the silence of the site, and, strangely, "rubbing the gravestones." Do New Hampshirites know that ghosts can attack even if Mommy and Daddy are nearby? Should someone tell them?

SEAWEED-ERS: In 2016, New Hampshire state representatives launched an initiative to help uncover obscure or outdated laws that should be repealed. Who did they turn to for help in this cause? Preteens. Representatives pitched the contest to middle schools across the state in hopes of inspiring students to engage in critical thinking and develop a better understanding of the legal system. The competition was a success: students from the Newport Middle High School in Concord, New Hampshire, discovered this law, hidden deep within the passages of the state's fish and game codes. Created in the 1700s to prevent farmers from gathering and hogging seaweed (which can be used as a fertilizer), this law forbids the collection of seaweed at night in order to give everyone "an equal chance to harvest." Impressed by the discovery, the state agreed to repeal the age-old law, granting dozens of middle schoolers a very strange yet impressive brag for their future college applications.

WOMEN WHO KILL: In 2017, the Republican-led legislature of New Hampshire amended the state law on homicide to include any fetuses that were aborted after twenty weeks. When the amendment, titled Senate Bill 66, passed, Republicans celebrated their win, but the party was short-lived. Soon after the legislation went through, people began to notice some strange phrasing in the bill . . . phrasing that technically suggested that pregnant women could commit homicide. Under the homicide and capital murder section, the amendment stated that "nothing in this section . . . shall apply to any act committed by the pregnant woman." Similar vague language also insinuated that "any act performed by a physician or other medical professional" was also allowable, making things like assisted suicides suddenly very legal. The Republicans scrambled to correct the error before any of these pregnant women seized on the opportunity to strike down any of their mortal enemies.

BLUE BUTTERFLIES: Planning on adding a blue butterfly to your taxidermy-insect collection? The state of New Hampshire won't allow it. Back in 1999, the Karner Blue Butterfly, a fluorescent indigo bug known for its wide wingspan and bright colors, was on the decline. Hoping to stop the population from dying out entirely, New Hampshire officials collected Karner eggs from around the state and began breeding them, reintroducing hundreds of blue butterflies back into the wild. They were able to do this because in 1992, these little flutterbugs became federally listed as endangered, making them protected under the Endangered Species Act of 1973. This means that it's illegal to possess, harm, harass, injure, or kill these precious gems or else risk legal repercussions. Though the numbers have fluctuated in the years since that declaration, the Karner population seems to be on the rise, which is good news for New Hampshire, who has dubbed the creature its official state butterfly.

HOTEL MOTEL HOLIDAY INN: On the run from the law? Here's a pro tip: don't try to stay at a hotel in the state of New Hampshire. If you do, you'll have to give them your real name because under the trade and commerce section of New Hampshire's general court legislature, any attempt to use a "false or fictitious name" is considered "prima facie evidence of intent to defraud." In other words, that alias you've been planning on using? Prince Alexander Hamilton Snollygoster? You can't. It's illegal. Breaking this 1969 rule can result in a misdemeanor or, worse, an embarrassing headline in a future newspaper piece titled "Stupid Reasons Criminals Got Busted."

NEW JERSEY
Have You Seen Our Shores?

BULLETPROOF: In the state of New Jersey, criminals are going to have to work a lot harder to, well, not die. According to one state code, wearing a bulletproof vest while committing an illegal act is prohibited. The actual text states that "use or wearing a body vest while engaged in the commission of, or an attempt to commit, or flight after committing or attempting to commit a crime of the first degree is a crime of the second degree." While the reasoning behind the measure is clear—anyone can agree that allowing robbers to make themselves bulletproof is probably a bad idea—the logic falls down a little bit when you remember that the people least likely to follow a law about making criminals unkillable . . . are criminals.

GAS ME UP: If you find yourself cruising around New Jersey in the middle of the night and your gas light blinks on, what should you do? Get gas, right? Unfortunately, it's not that simple. The Garden State is one of the only ones in the country that prohibits motorists from pumping their own gas thanks to the 1949 Retail Gasoline Dispensing Safety Act that insists "it is in the public interest that gasoline station operators have the control needed over [pumping gas] to ensure compliance with appropriate safety procedures, including turning off vehicle engines and refraining from smoking while fuel is dispensed." In essence, New Jerseyans cannot fill their gas tanks on their own because they cannot be trusted. So, when you pull up to that aforementioned gas station only find that the attendants have all gone home and locked the pumps, just remember that this was done to protect you.

IT'S BEGINNING TO LOOK A LOT LIKE CHRISTMAS: Good luck trying to sneak up on New Jerseyans, Santa. One state statute prevents the use of sleighs unless "there are a sufficient number of bells attached to the horse's harness to give warning of its approach." The law's origin is unclear, which begs the question: Did Santa once ruffle the feathers of some poor Garden State citizen by accidentally scaring them to death, causing them to complain to the local authorities about the unlawful use of sleighs in the city? Did a Karen cause this?

WHAT DID THE FOX SAY?: New Jersey doesn't care how cute that red fox trapped in your basement is—you can't release it back into the wild. A state law from 2009 forbids the "liberation" of foxes within the state and carries a penalty of one hundred dollars per fox. A similar law also applies to coyotes, which suggests that the measure was likely put in place to protect residents from these unpredictable wild animals. So, what do you do with the fox that wandered into your cellar and is now burrowing into your nice hardwood? No idea. Domesticate it, maybe. Regular pets are so last year.

DRUNK DINNER GUESTS: You know what they say: Don't come to dinner if you can't hold your liquor. That's a phrase, right? Well, it should be, at least in the town of Mount Laurel, New Jersey. This tiny township does not allow residents to get drunk and annoy others in their homes, no matter the occasion. Section § 109-1 of their official legislature states that "no person shall, within the limits of the Township of Mount Laurel be intoxicated or drunk or disorderly in any public omnibus, street, highway, thoroughfare or on any sidewalk or in any private house, home or in any boardinghouse, store, restaurant or other private, public or quasi-public place or house to the annoyance of any person." Does this mean that citizens of Mount Laurel can sue their significant other for stumbling home after a night out and vomiting all over the newly constructed IKEA couch, even though the bathroom was like, right there? We'll leave that to their discretion.

SHOW KIDS: Show moms in New Jersey are in for a shock when they read this strangely specific measure. Under the state of New Jersey's child labor laws and regulations, children cannot be forced to "publicly perform" certain acts unless they've been properly trained. Such acts include wrestling, boxing, tightrope walking, horseback riding, and a slew of other things that kids shouldn't be doing anyway, if we're being totally honest. The measure is intended to protect the lives and health of the children which, judging from the mental gymnastics these "show kids" have to go through on a daily basis, is probably a good call.

NEW YORK
I'm Walkin' Here

MASKED: Are you a US citizen preparing to invoke your constitutional right to protest? Did you have Halloween plans to dress up like some mythical animal? Are you a working clown preparing for an upscale birthday party gig? If any of these apply to you, then you are most likely investing in a mask of some sort. And if that's the case, and you live in the state of New York, you're also, in turn, about to break the law. Here's why: in the 1800s, in retaliation to a drop in wheat prices, farmers across the state of New York began to dress up like Native Americans and attack police. The incidents got so bad that the N.Y. Penal Law 240.35(4) was passed, which prohibited "being masked or in any manner disguised by unusual or unnatural attire or facial alteration." (The exceptions to the rule were masquerades and police-sanctioned events.)

While this may seem silly, the law actually came in handy a few decades later with the rise of the KKK and other terrorist organizations that use face coverings to shield their identities. As a result, the state of New York kept the ruling in place, right up until May 2020 when the spread of the novel coronavirus COVID-19 forced the widespread use of masks and caused the law to be repealed.

TIGER KING: Dreaming of becoming the next Tiger King? You might have to keep your ambitions under wraps, at least on social media. In 2014, Governor Andrew Cuomo banned "direct contact between the public and big cats . . . including, but not limited to, allowing a photograph to be taken without a permanent physical barrier designed to prevent physical contact between the public and big cats," among other things.

Why does such a law need to exist, you ask? Ask the men of New York State. According to some sources, this measure was enacted thanks to a rise in men on dating sites taking selfies with circus and zoo animals and posting them on dating apps in order to attract women. Animal advocates, including the (now infamous) Carol Baskin of *Tiger King*, condemned the trend and urged men to take photos with domestic felines instead.

A FOR ADULTERY: When you're caught cheating in New York, your significant other can do more than just throw your clothes out the window—they can sue. According to Section 255.17 of the New York state penal law, "a person is guilty of adultery when he engages in sexual intercourse with another person at a time when he has a living spouse, or the other person has a living spouse" and can be punished with up to ninety days in jail or a five-hundred-dollar fine. Although you might think that a ruling like this would result in an overwhelming number of cases (there is still no cure for cheaters, after all), since its inception in the 1970s, there have only been around a dozen people officially charged with the crime. Someone call Hester Prynne.

SPIT TAKE: You've got to be spittin' me. In the state of New York, the law says that "no person shall spit upon a sidewalk of a street or place, or on a floor, wall or stairway of any public or private building or premises used in common by the public, or in or on any public transportation facility." This makes sense, of course. Not only is spitting legally considered harassment in some places (including the Big Apple) but it's downright gross. Public transportation is icky enough without saliva dribbling down its aisles. Give commuters a break, huh?

FLIRT NO MORE: Anyone who has ever been to New York City has likely been a victim of catcalling, an unfortunate practice whereby ogling men make inappropriate comments toward female passersby in hopes of getting their numbers or, at the very least, their fleeting attention. It might be surprising to know, then, that this very common practice was once nearly banned. In the early 1900s, as men returned from war feeling all hot and bothered, they began to increasingly prey on young women—offering them rides home or boldly professing their attraction in hopes of picking up a date.

In fact, the "flirting" problem became so severe, it sparked a wave of "anti-flirting" chapters across the country, composed of women who had become frustrated by these groups of predatory men. One chapter based in Washington even went so far as to publish a list of "chapter rules" in the *Washington Post* to educate the masses on the pillars of their "anti-flirt movement." The list included items like "Don't wink—a flutter of one eye may cause a tear in the other!" and "Don't let elderly men with an eye to a flirtation pat you on the shoulder and take a fatherly interest in you. Those are usually the kind who want to forget they are fathers."

All of this tension came to a head in 1902 when one state assemblyman named William Bennett introduced a new bill that stated "any person who is intoxicated in a public place, or who shall by any offensive or disorderly act or language, annoy or interfere with any person or persons in any place, or with the passengers of any public stage, railroad car, or ferryboat, or who shall disturb or offend the occupants of such conveyance by any disorderly act or language or display, although such conduct may not amount to an assault or battery, shall be guilty of a misdemeanor." Though it's not clear whether the law actually went through or if it is still in effect, its existence speaks volumes about the Empire State and the eye-roll energy of the women within it.

FERRET FRIENDS: What's bigger than a mouse, smaller than a rat, and banned in the city of New York? The wide-eyed, long-bodied, undeniably stinky animals known as ferrets. They were banned in 1999 by Mayor Rudy Giuliani, who believed that the animals could spread rabies and were therefore dangerous. When the city council tried to overturn his ruling in 2001, voting with a twenty-six to thirteen majority, he vetoed the measure and released a memorandum titled "Talking Points Against the Legalization of Ferrets" that insisted ferrets were "naturally inclined to do harm" and that they would "travel through tiny holes in walls" and spread diseases to the city's residents.

Though Rudy's tenure ended in 2001, city officials have continued to uphold the measure, despite efforts from animal advocates to reconsider. Ferret lovers got close in 2015 but failed to overturn the ruling, thanks to some voters who expressed fear that the "unique skeletal structure of ferrets [would allow] them to squeeze through very small crevices." Foiled again, ferrets.

FAMILY FEUD: In 2020, New York City was named the sixth most expensive city in the world. As a result, it is common to find residents living with strange combinations of old college roommates, exes, and professional harmonica players that they found on Craigslist at the last minute. What some people don't know is that, according to §27–2075 of the city's housing maintenance code, doing so is technically forbidden. The code states that it is "illegal for more than three unrelated people to live in an apartment or a house" in the Big Apple, a rule that, thanks to the city's unwieldy rent prices and crippling housing crisis, is almost impossible to follow. Thankfully, the law is rarely enforced—it turns out knocking on the doors of over eight million people to investigate their roommate situation isn't as feasible as lawmakers may have thought.

PENNSYLVANIA
The OG Colony

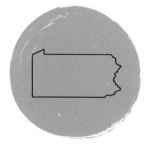

BABY BLUES: Parenting is hard. All the mommy blogs say so. If that's the case, why aren't there more opportunities to get rid of those pesky kids? Shouldn't it be legal to, say, barter your children away for something more valuable, like money or a free year of Spotify Premium? Pennsylvania doesn't think so. Hidden in its state legislature, under offenses against the family, government officials have made clear that "trading, bartering, buying, selling, or dealing in infant children" is illegal. But don't worry. If your children are really driving you up the wall and there is just no other choice but to exchange them, you'll only be hit with a misdemeanor charge—a small price to pay for peace and quiet.

TROUTY MOUTH: In the state of Pennsylvania, you're allowed to use just about anything to catch a fish. A fishing rod? Of course. A bucket? Definitely. A sawed-off can of Pepsi you found in the back of your pickup truck? You bet! There is, however, one fishing method that is off-limits in these parts: chomping a fish in your mouth. In fact, using any part of your body to catch a fish is illegal in Pennsylvania, per rules set by the fish and boat commission. Doing so will land you a one-hundred-dollar fine and some very, very bad breath.

SIXTH SENSE: Northeasterners put up with a lot of things (six never-ending months of winter, rabid sports fans, and clueless out-of-towners), but witchery is not one of them. The Pennsylvania general assembly has no tolerance for "fortune telling," an umbrella term used for general acts of magic or superstition. Under title 18, it states: "A person is guilty of a misdemeanor of the third degree if he pretends for gain or lucre, to tell fortunes or predict future events, by cards, tokens, the inspection of the head or hands of any person, or by the age of anyone, or by consulting the movements of the heavenly bodies, or in any other manner." The title also forbids charms, necromancy, or incantations of any kind including hexes, love potions, or predictions involving marriage or money, so don't let anyone see you using a cootie catcher.

GIVE IT A SHOT: A typical paintball flies out of the barrel at 240 feet per second. That's enough to take your breath away and leave a purple welt on your skin that your mom will be nervously asking about for weeks. That's why Pennsylvania has made it illegal to shoot strangers with paintball guns. The law states that "an individual may not discharge or fire a paintball gun or paintball marker at a person who is not participating in paintball games or paintball-related recreational activities" in order to prevent innocent residents from suddenly thinking they've been shot after walking out to retrieve their mail and getting hit with a faceful of high-speed magenta dye.

CHILD'S PLAY: Pennsylvania residents seem very concerned about their bathrooms. One law states that "there shall be at least one bathtub or shower for every six children." Another claims that "bar soap is not permitted unless there is a separate bar clearly labeled for each child." But perhaps the most interesting law is the one demanding that "a child's bedroom may not be more than two-hundred feet from a bathtub or shower and a toilet." You know, because anything further may result in an emergency trip to the laundry machine from an accidental PJ-wetting situation.

RHODE ISLAND
Small but Mighty

DUEL IT OUT: In 2018, Rhode Island lawmaker John Edwards decided to clean up his state's legislature by introducing dozens of bills that would repeal obscure laws like this one, which says that "every person who shall voluntarily engage in a duel with any dangerous weapon, to the hazard of life, shall be imprisoned," and "every person who shall

challenge another to fight a duel with any dangerous weapon, to the hazard of life, and every person who shall accept a challenge to fight such duel, although no duel be fought, shall be imprisoned" The twist? Edwards' 2018 efforts failed. As it turns out, some of the original laws, including the 1798 prohibition on dueling, are still being used today. So frequently, in fact, that the move to strike it from the books was rejected in both legislative chambers. Alexander Hamilton may have died in 1804 but his swashbuckling legacy has clearly lived on in the hearts of New Englanders.

GIVE ME A HAND: Thank God Mike Tyson wasn't in Rhode Island when he bit off Evander Holyfield's ear: he'd be looking at one to twenty years in prison. According to a state law (RI Gen L § 11-29-1) dating back to 1896, it is illegal to bite off the limb or appendage of another person. The statute also prohibits the slitting of the nose, the removal of the eye, or the disabling of any limbs. What's striking about the measure is the use of the word "voluntarily," which suggests that any of the above is applicable if you can invent a convincing enough defense about how you ended up accidentally biting off your brother's nose or slicing off your neighbor's ankle. Get creative.

WHOA, HORSEY: Back in the 1800s, leisure activities were a fairly new concept. Baseball was on the rise, soft drinks were being introduced to the masses, and the success of the printing press spurned the creation of pulpy magazines and cheap newspapers. If you didn't have access to such activities, you had to make your own fun, like the handful of Rhode Islanders who decided to race horses on highways, forcing officials to create a law in 1896 that states: "Every person who shall drive any horse over any of the public highways, for the purpose of racing or trying the speed of the horse, shall be fined not more than twenty dollars ($20.00) or imprisoned not exceeding ten (10) days" (RI Gen L § 11-22-11). While we have since developed more sophisticated tastes (now we watch cars race for fun instead of animals), the law remains on the books . . . just in case.

HELLO, GOVERNOR: Were impersonators a problem in the 1800s? Were there Thomas Edison look-alikes walking around, juggling light bulbs and phonographs? Were men with beards roaming the streets, calling themselves Abe Lincoln to pick up chicks? Were there people trotting around on horses with rimless glasses, trying to pass themselves off as Teddy Roosevelt? These are all valid questions, especially considering the existence of an 1896 law that prohibits anyone from acting like government officials by exercising "any of the legislative, executive, or ministerial functions of the office of governor, lieutenant-governor, senator, member of the house of representatives, secretary of state, attorney general, or general treasurer." The punishment for breaking this law is life imprisonment, so we can assume that something crazy must have happened to make this rule a reality.

PHONE AN ENEMY: If you've ever wanted to bellow into a receiver at the unhelpful customer service agent on the other end or cuss out one of your parents over the phone for their frustrating political views, we have some bad news. In the Ocean State, anyone who uses "any threatening, vulgar, indecent, obscene, or immoral language over the telephone" shall be guilty of a misdemeanor and will be subject to a hefty fine or up to one year in prison. So next time you have the urge to give someone a piece of your mind, just remember how uncomfortable orange jumpsuits are and how it would be in your best interest to avoid them.

WHEN PIGS FLY: These days, when someone says the word pig, the first thing you think of is bacon, pork, or those teacup pigs that you see on the internet wearing bowties and posing for photoshoots. Back in the 1900s, though, pigs were an important asset to farmers, especially in Rhode Island. While they were used to produce the aforementioned meaty goods, they were also helpful in creating sustainable farming practices—back then, pig farmers would make contracts with local communities whereby they would pick up food scraps from nearby businesses at the end of the day and bring it back to the farm to feed it to the pigs, thus preventing food waste. Such practices made pigs a valuable commodity in the Ocean State, so much so that officials drafted up a law in 1896 preventing the theft of "any domestic animal" including swine, horses, and poultry. Another law from 1909 reinforces this, stating that "every person who breaks and enters, or enters in the nighttime without breaking, any building or enclosure in which are kept or confined any kind of poultry, with intent to steal any of the poultry, shall be punished by imprisonment." Basically, keep your paws off the pigs and chickens.

VERMONT
Every Day Is Flannel Friday

GIRAFFE GAFFE: If you're planning on walking your pet giraffe around Vermont, you best bring a leash: one law prohibits citizens from tying giraffes to telephone poles. Funny, right? Unfortunately, the phrasing of the law is a bit misleading. According to the original measure, which was written in the 1880s, "a person who willfully and maliciously breaks the glass about a streetlamp . . . or fastens a horse or animal thereto, shall be imprisoned not more than three months or fined not more than $50.00, or both." Which is to say, it's illegal to tie any animal to a streetlamp in Vermont. And because giraffes are technically animals and fall into that vague category, the law isn't a total lie, just a tiny distortion of the truth.

THERE REALLY IS A GOD: Atheists, listen up. Denying the existence of God in the state of Vermont is, technically, against the law—one that was created in the eighteenth century when prejudice against atheists was rampant. This all changed around 1979 when the blasphemy law was repealed in favor of religious freedom and free speech, or whatever.

CLOTHESLINE ENERGY: Here's a fact that's rarely talked about: laundry pollutes. Washer-dryers eat up energy like a starved college student returning home for winter break, and some socially conscious crowds are getting tired of it. Thankfully, an unlikely champion has emerged: clotheslines. Though banned in many parts of the country for being "unsightly" to neighboring homes, clotheslines are making a comeback in some states, including Florida, Colorado, Hawaii, Maine,

Maryland, and, unsurprisingly, Vermont for being a cost-effective and eco-friendly way to dry garments. In 2009, as more and more communities were starting to embrace the use of these stringy tools, one Vermont resident, Lyman Orton, decided to take the clotheslines movement to the next level by launching a Right to Dry initiative. Citing Vermont's "heritage of practicality, frugality, and common sense," Orton put forward a bill (Senate Bill 18) that outlawed the prohibition of clotheslines by arguing that they were a form of "solar energy." Thanks to his efforts, Vermonters can now let their cotton-knit bedding flap freely in the wind any time they want.

HOLD YOUR HORSES: First mentioned in *The Aeneid*, the story of the Trojan Horse goes as follows: back in 1184 B.C., Greek soldiers, who had long sought to infiltrate the city of Troy, came up with an ingenious idea: they would build a large wooden horse and present it to the city as a "victory offering." Then, when the citizens accepted the gift and rolled it into their town center, the Greek soldiers hiding in the horse's hollow belly would slip out and take over the city from the inside out. Centuries later, some places are still haunted by this idea, including Vermont. In a 2012 list of Vermont statutes, it's written that a person cannot own a "painted or disguised" horse or "fraudulently [represent] a horse to be another from what it really is." The rule, it seems, was created to prevent farmers from presenting their animals as special breeds that would earn them monetary premiums from agricultural companies and the like. It makes you wonder just how many people are out there painting donkeys dark and trying to pass them off as Black Stallions.

FAKE TEETH: If you're a woman looking to buy dentures in Vermont, you best get your husband's permission first. Thanks to an antiquated Vermont supreme court ruling, women in need of false teeth must first present their dentist with a written note from their husbands. This strange (and hardly enforced) requirement came about in 1856 when a man named Leonard Gilman was called to the state's supreme court by his wife's dentist, Willis Andrus, after the wife requested "a plate of mineral teeth" and then never paid up. The case (*Gilman v. Andrus*) ruled that "artificial teeth must be considered necessities, and for that reason the husband is liable for payment when they have been furnished his wife, particularly if she retains them with his knowledge, and he has given the dentist who supplied them reason to believe, from previous conversation with him, that she was authorized to contract for them." In other words, husbands must give dentists some sort of signal that their wives are allowed to get fake teeth.

THE SOUTHEAST
Swamplandia

With fourteen states, the Southeast is a bit of a beast. Its northern corridor is filled with rolling hills, forested mountains, and sandy tourist beaches, while its southern corridor is host to wetlands, swamps, and Florida people—a wild, unpredictable species. But don't worry, they don't bite. In fact, no one in this corner of the United States will. From the aspiring Tennessee country stars to the football-loving college students, the people of this region are known for their Southern charm and colorful personalities. So long as you don't make any comments about their sweet tea recipe, Southeastern folk will welcome you with open arms and send you on your way with a stack of cornbread, a new appreciation for Appalachia, and a fresh coat of sweat. (It's humid; you've been warned.)

ALABAMA
We Killed a Mockingbird

OK, JESUS: It's true—Jesus and a chalice of wine would be a great costume—but if you live in Alabama, you're going to need to find an alternative. According to Alabama's criminal code, Section 13A-14-4: "Whoever, being in a public place, fraudulently pretends by garb or outward array to be a minister of any religion, or nun, priest, rabbi or other member of the clergy, is guilty of a misdemeanor and, upon conviction, shall be punished by a fine not exceeding $500.00 or confinement in the county jail for not more than one year, or by both such fine and imprisonment." Not sure who out there is pretending to be a pastor or why, but your days of tomfoolery have come to an end. More accurately, they came to an end in 1965, when this law was passed.

BEAR WITH ME: Axe throwing and skeet shooting are some of Alabama's well-known pastimes, but there's another, more absurd activity that these Dixieland residents love: bear wrestling. Since the 1930s, men have been participating in bear-wrestling matches in dark, smoky basements to show off their machismo. During these matches, defanged, declawed bears would be dragged into the "ring" (a.k.a. a circle of drunken bar patrons), secured to a chain leash, and forced to battle opponents with names like The Purple Flash and The Country Rover. While these men would sometimes hash it out for the money—some places offered a dollar per every minute spent in the ring—others would do it for the sheer pride of being able to say, "I fought a six-hundred-pound bear."

If you're thinking, "Well that doesn't sound very fun for the bear," you're correct. Animal advocates over the years have criticized this practice, claiming that bears cannot consent to being tossed in the ring with fame-hungry, roughhousing men. They also pointed out the poor conditions that these creatures were being subjected to; many were often kept in small trailers and fed poor diets while being touted across the country as a lucrative sideshow act. So, in 1996, following a series of famous bear matches hosted by Terrible Ted at the Ponderosa Club in Alabama, the state senate banned the practice by a unanimous vote. Thanks to these efforts, bear wrestling faded out over the years and, in 2015, when the act was repealed (along with a handful of other antiquated laws), no one even batted an eye.

SUNDAY DOMINOES: Sundays were made for worshipping the Lord, not for wasting time on surprisingly mundane tabletop games. That's what the Alabama legislature says, anyway. Section 13A-12-1 of the Alabama code very specifically states that children cannot be compelled to perform any laborious activity on Sundays, including shooting, hunting, racing, card playing, or "gaming," which includes dominos and other childhood pastimes. Doing so can result in a large fine or three months of hard labor for the county. So, listen to the experts and just chill on Sundays, OK?

BLIND LEADING THE BLIND: You think you're a good driver? Well, have you ever operated a car while blindfolded? I didn't think so. Unfortunately, if you live in sweet home Alabama, you're never going to get the chance. Section 32-5A-53 of Alabama's legislature states that "no person shall drive a vehicle when it is loaded, or when there are in the front seat such a number of persons as to obstruct the view of the driver to the front or sides of the vehicle or as to interfere with the driver's control over the driving mechanism of the vehicle." Though likely created by frustrated parents who wanted their kids to stop jokingly reaching over from the back seat and covering their eyes, the law is so vague that driving with any obstruction, blindfolds included, is fair game.

WIPED: Alabama sees a problem with, well, not being able to see—while driving, at least. The state requires every car in the area to be equipped with "a device for cleaning rain, snow or other moisture from the windshield, which device shall be so constructed as to be controlled or operated by the driver of the vehicle." Does this "device" necessarily have to be a rigid plastic wiper? Technically, no. You could fasten two swords to your windshields and manually swipe them back and forth whenever it snows, and as long as it eliminates the obstruction, you're within your rights.

ARKANSAS
God, Guns, and Football

SAY IT RIGHT: Though it's not technically illegal to mispronounce the state's name, it's still highly discouraged, according to Section 1-4-105 of the Arkansas code, which outlines in great detail exactly how the name is to be pronounced: "Be it therefore resolved by both houses of the General Assembly, that the only true pronunciation of the name of the state, in the opinion of this body, is that it should be pronounced in three (3) syllables, with the final s silent, the a in each syllable with the Italian sound, and the accent on the first and last syllables. The pronunciation with the accent on the second syllable with the sound of a in man and the sounding of the terminal s is an innovation to be discouraged." You heard it here first.

SACRED SANDWICHES: Little Rock, Arkansas, has a big problem with those who disrespect sandwiches. Buried deep within their state code, in a tiny section under offenses involving public peace, it is noted that "no person shall sound the horn on a vehicle at any place where cold drinks or sandwiches are served after 9:00 p.m." This raises more questions than it answers, like how did this law come to be? Did a hangry Little Rock resident provoke a sandwich shop owner by idling outside of their closed store and furiously honking, forcing the owner to reluctantly reopen for a minute in order to make the pesky customer a BLT and send them on their way? Did some lazy resident order a cold drink, then rush off to their car in hopes that the owner would deliver it to their window when it was done? And, when the owner didn't, did that lazy person start obnoxiously honking and flashing their lights, as if to say, "Hey! Don't you dare forget about me! I paid for that Philly Cheesesteak, and I expect to get it!"

DON'T POKE THE BEAR: Since the 1950s, Arkansas has been trying to preserve their dwindling bear population by implementing strict hunting laws and crafting specific rules meant to protect the fuzzy creatures. One such law states that "it is unlawful to shine artificial lights from any public road, or on any wildlife management area, for viewing or locating wildlife." This seemingly standard rule has been twisted out of context on the internet, creating the rumor that it is illegal to wake a sleeping bear for the purpose of taking a picture. While this law does restrict shining an artificial light on wildlife in order to view them" it seems unlikely that unwarranted bear selfies were enough of a problem in Arkansas that lawmakers would feel obliged to take action. But how should I know? I don't live there.

FLIRTING WITH DANGER: Is it true that flirting on the streets of Little Rock, Arkansas, is illegal? Yes and no. In the late 1800s, "houses of ill-fame" like brothels were concerning to residents, who viewed the practice of prostitution as morally questionable. In 1913, Mayor Charles Edward Taylor and his Little Rock vice commission ordered the shutdown of these businesses across the city and demanded that sex workers skip town or find new business.

While many of these institutions did, in fact, shut down, their members stuck around. With nowhere to go, they took their business to the streets, to the dismay of Mayor Taylor, who rushed to pass a law that would restrict their illicit behavior. The law stated that "it shall be unlawful for any person to attract or to endeavor to attract the attention of any person of the opposite sex, upon or traveling along any of the sidewalks, streets or public ways of the City of Little Rock, by staring at, winking at, coughing at or whistling at such person, with the intent, or in any way calculated to annoy, or to attempt to flirt with any such person." It was the loose interpretation of this ordinance, which has since disappeared from Arkansas' state code, that led to this absurd-sounding rule against flirting in Little Rock.

KEEP IT MOO-VING: In Little Rock, you cannot walk your cow between certain hours. Why? For the same reason that running through the streets banging on pots and pans is discouraged: because it's annoying. The law, which prohibits cow-walking between 10:00 p.m. and 4:00 a.m. (among other windows), specifies that cows cannot wear bells after 9:00 p.m.

DELAWARE
Shine Bright Like a Diamond

R-RATED: Want to watch an R-rated movie in Delaware? Get a room. No, really. In Delaware, outdoor movie theaters are not allowed to play R-rated films. Why? In 1949, Delaware's first drive-in theater, The Brandywine Drive-in, opened to rave reviews, sparking a boom in outdoor cinemas. But nothing good lasts forever, and by the time the 1970s rolled around, these once-beloved drive-ins were crumbling. To stay in business, some theaters began playing adult films, which irked families living nearby who didn't want their children watching big-screen boobies from their windows. By 1974, Delaware had decided that it had enough and passed a law (11 Del.C. § 1366) banning movies "not suitable for minors."

Delaware's prudence didn't last long, though. In 1975, a Supreme Court case involving an outdoor cinema in Florida (why is it always

Florida . . .) ruled that banning movies with an R-rating was unconstitutional. Despite this though, Delaware has left the law in its state code, though it's rarely enforced. It would be difficult to, anyway: Delaware's last drive-in closed in 2008.

TAKE A LEG: For some people, selling their organs on the black market is a viable way to pay off debts. Desperate times call for desperate measures, yadda yadda yadda. Not in Delaware. In this little Diamond State, pawnbrokers are forbidden from accepting artificial legs (Delaware Code, § 2307). So that means no matter how much money you spend on custom-designed Etsy COVID-19 masks, you won't be able to get that money back by trading in your leg or arm or any other limb, for that matter.

LATE-NIGHT TAILGATE: Delaware is not known for their sports, as much as they might want to be. And yet, that hasn't stopped them from adopting sports-related laws in an attempt to feel like a Big Ten state. One such 1980 law in the town of Fenwick Island, Delaware, forbids tailgating from 12:00 a.m. to 6:00 a.m. (§ 116-6). Abandon those dreams you have of sipping an ice-cold Bud Lite in the back of a pickup truck at 1:00 a.m. with a discarded foam finger cushioning your body from the rigid flatbed metal. Get rid of them. They're not going to happen. Goodbye.

SABBATH SUNDAY: On March 2, 1941, Delaware's state attorney general James Morford did something bold: he enforced a law. More specifically, he enforced a 1795 blue law stating that "one cannot break the Sabbath" for any reason. Why? Because a few weeks prior, the state house of representatives vetoed an amendment that would have given communities the right to individually decide how blue laws should be implemented. As a result, this "no breaking the Sabbath" rule remained a statewide law, which angered Morford, who believed the rule was unenforceable on such a large scale and desecrated the public's trust in the law. In one public statement, he argued: "We have thereby created uncertainty as to what an honest citizen may or may not do, but we have created a situation where he may do an act one day and be apparently a law-abiding citizen while the same act next day may subject him to arrest . . . But the worse feature is that by substituting the discretion of a man for the mandate of the law we have gone far to destroy respect for all law and have opened a door for graft and corruption in public office."

So, what did Morford do? He decided to prove just how ridiculous such a statewide ruling was. To do this, Morford decided to arbitrarily fine and arrest over five hundred people in Wilmington, Delaware, one Sunday. He rounded up anyone committing non-church related activities, including milkmen, taxi drivers, and hotel patrons who dared to have dinner in their building's restaurants. Morford even fined a local pastor who had been using a radio broadcast to advertise his morning sermon.

Crazy? Yes. Effective? Surprisingly. A week after this Blue Massacre incident, the state legislature finally passed a reformed blue law bill that eased up on some of these crazy restrictions and state prosecutors dropped all pending cases against these unruly lawbreakers.

FUR BABIES: Here's a riddle for you: What's PETA's favorite US state? Answer: Delaware, of course. According to one section of the state of Delaware code, anyone who "knowingly or recklessly sells, barters or offers for sale . . . the fur or hair of a domestic dog or cat or any product made in whole or in part from the fur or hair of a domestic dog or cat" is subject to a misdemeanor. Anyone caught selling coats, hats, furry vests, etc. that were made even in part with animal fur are also subject to a $2,500 fine and a ban on owning any animals for fifteen years after conviction. So, if you want to hold onto your fur baby, try not to profit off their hair. This should go without saying but . . . here we are.

FLORIDA

If It Was on the News, It Was Probably Florida

HURRICANE PARTY: While Florida may be called the Sunshine State, a more fitting name for it might be the Hurricane State. This sliver of land dangles off the edge of the country like a hangnail and is surrounded by a beautiful, dolphin-filled ocean. The downside to this is that it has become the perfect target for tropical storms, which scoop up the nearby water and dump it right back onto the mainland in big, flashy weather events called hurricanes.

When this happens, Floridians have a few options. They can either take the first flight out of the state to avoid the watery onslaught, or they can hunker down and prepare to ride out the storm. And what better way to cope with an extended traumatic event than alcohol? Unsurprisingly, Floridians—who are famously either college students or heat-seaking senior citizens—have developed a reputation for throwing "hurricane parties" whereby friends and families gather around to drink while storms rage on around them. In an effort to curb this behavior, a statute was put in place in 1974 that gives the governor of Florida the right to suspend alcohol sales during a state of emergency. While it was a good thought, the governor forgot how adaptable Floridians are because now, instead of buying their drinks drinks the day a hurricane hits, they buy wine in bulk and hoard it like middle-aged moms.

DOT-COM DOOM: In 2013, Florida lieutenant governor Jennifer Carroll was caught red-handed using a line of internet cafes tied to a veteran charity as a front for illegal gambling; with her help these cafes raked in 290 million dollars over the course of a few years. In an effort to quash the scandal and prevent future wrongdoing, the state governor Rick Scott hastily passed a bill that banned internet cafes. In doing so, thanks to the law's vague wording, he also technically banned all computers and smartphones in the process. The law defined slot machines as "any machine or device or system or network of devices," a designation so broad that digital devices like laptops and iPhones qualify.

Lawmakers caught the mistake after Consuelo Zapata, the owner of a cafe providing internet services to migrants, filed a complaint, noting that the bill was, in its current form, very unconstitutional. Florida lawmakers, however, did not see the problem, claiming that they would never interpret the law that literally. Only time will tell.

BAD DOG: Some people put up a Beware of Dog sign in their yard to scare robbers away. Others do it as a joke to mock their feisty five-pound chihuahua. But some put up these signs because their dog is actually dangerous. If you fall into the last category and your dog ends up biting someone on your property, there is some good news: you're off the hook. According to one Florida statute, "The owner of any dog that bites any person while such person is on or in a public place, or lawfully on or in a private place, including the property of the owner of the dog, is liable for damages suffered by persons bitten . . . However, the owner is not liable, except as to a person under the age of six, or unless the damages are proximately caused by a negligent act or omission of the owner, if at the time of any such injury the owner had displayed in a prominent place on his or her premises a sign easily readable including the words 'Bad Dog.'" Congrats, Cujo. You're free to live another day.

PRETTY KITTY: We've all heard of a guard dog, but what about a guard cat? One town in Florida seems to have a problem with protective kitties: in Destin, Florida's code of ordinances, not only does it state that owners cannot encourage their animals to bite or attack another, but also it states that it is unlawful "for any dog or cat, when unprovoked, to approach or chase any person in an apparent attitude of attack or in a vicious or terrorizing manner, such dog or cat shall be deemed a 'bad dog' or 'bad cat'" (Section 4-8). If you dare to own one of these vicious, stranger-chasing felines, make sure you keep a leash on it.

UP, UP, AND AWAY: Remember that shot from the Disney Pixar film *Up* featuring a house hitched to five hundred floating balloons? Well, don't get any ideas. Thanks to one 2011 Florida statute, it's illegal to intentionally release more than ten balloons within a twenty-four-hour period.

PREGGY PIGGY: Pregnant women deserve our respect for many reasons, including the fact that they can endure nine months of morning sickness, aching backs, and sleeplessness. Why don't we extend the same reverence to pregnant pigs? Well, in Florida, they do. While the state by no means a PETA paradise, they have implemented measures to protect their barn animals, including the pink oinking ones. An article in the Florida constitution prohibits the "cruel confinement" of pregnant pigs. It states that "no person shall confine a pig during pregnancy in a cage, crate or other enclosure, or tether a pregnant pig, on a farm so that the pig is prevented from turning around freely." Give those new moms room to breathe.

GEORGIA
More Than Just Peaches

I'M ON A BOAT: If you've ever joked about selling all of your worldly belongings and living on a boat in the middle of the ocean, you might have to reconsider. In the early 1990s, boaters looking for a place to dock their vessels would go down to the Altamaha River and plunk them in the water, leaving them there for weeks and weeks at a time. The area's residents became concerned about this boat graveyard—which they viewed as destructive to the environment and, frankly, an eyesore—and made a fuss to the authorities, prompting the state of Georgia to enact this law. Needless to say, it didn't go over well—boaters viewed the move as unfriendly and aggressive to the boating community and took their business elsewhere, forcing Georgia to relax the time frame to ninety days. This seems reasonable—if you're spending more than ninety days on a boat in a given year, you might want to reevaluate what it is that's scaring you away from the land. A psychotic ex? An overbearing mother? An accidental murder? It's OK. We've all been there.

CHICKEN FRIED: Believe it or not, peaches are not Georgia's largest crop: it's chicken. The credit for that goes to a man named Jesse Jewel who, in 1922, pioneered a new poultry producing system that used vertical integration to boost farmer profits and mass-produce poultry products on a scale never before seen. Though he died in 1962, he left behind a legacy, one that put Georgia on the agricultural map. Decades later, that reputation still stands, so much so that laws have started materializing around this beloved bird, including one that forbids anyone from eating fried chicken with a fork. The 1961 ordinance was originally created as a gimmick to promote Gainesville, Georgia's status as the "Poultry Capital of the World," but it has since become a sort of inside joke for residents of the state, who fondly stab at their dinners in public, hoping to have a little bit of naughty fun.

DEAD BIRD: In the mob, when you want to send a message to someone that they've done something wrong, you might send them a bloody pig's head. In Conyers, Georgia, you would leave a dead bird on their lawn, partially because it's eerily specific, but also because the internet says it's illegal and what's more intimidating than a rule-breaker? But here's the thing: the internet's not always right. Do a little digging, and you'll find that the real law is a bit broader. Per Section 11-3-7 of the Conyers code of ordinances, "No person shall place any dead animal upon his premises or upon the premises of any other person or allow any dead animal to remain upon his premises or permit any dead animal belonging to the person to remain upon the premises of another without disposing of same or causing the animal to be properly removed or disposed of within twenty-four hours." Why, then, do so many sites point to birds specifically? Well, it might be because the city of Conyers has a special reverence for birds: one of its other ordinances has declared the city a sanctuary for birds and forbids anyone from knowingly killing them.

WATCH YOUR MOUTH: Respect the dead. In the state of Georgia, it is illegal to use "profane, indecent, or obscene language in the presence of a dead human body, or within the immediate hearing of the family or relatives of a deceased, whose body has not yet been interred or otherwise disposed" (§ 43-18-46). While this rule was directed toward aspiring funeral directors (running your mouth in front of a corpse can squash your chances of obtaining a funeral home license), the phrasing is just vague enough to inspire confusion and maybe a few laughs.

WELL, THAT'S ANNOYING: In Columbus, Georgia, it is considered unlawful to "sell, or keep on hand for sale, or offer for sale, or use, or possess in the city or its police district, any substances or articles commonly known as itch powder, sneeze powder, stink bombs or similar substances or articles." Basically, anything that your little brother might consider "cool" is a no-no.

KENTUCKY
Giddy Up

SNAKE CHARMED: There is a centuries-old Christian tradition whereby preachers handle venomous snakes during church service to show their followers how God protects them from danger. This would be a miraculous feat, except for the fact that it doesn't always work. Believe it or not, snakes aren't very well-tempered, especially when they're being draped across somebody's sweaty shoulders and paraded around like a fashion accessory, so the number of people that die from snakebites on a yearly basis has remained pretty steady. Despite this, there are approximately 125 churches in the United States—mostly in the Appalachia region—that continue to put on a show with these snappy creatures.

Kentucky is one of those places. In fact, the use of snakes in the area has become so problematic that the state implemented a law in 1942 forbidding the use of reptiles in religious services altogether. Has this stopped religious leaders from cuddling with these angsty reptiles? Not even a little bit. Preachers across the state continue to employ venomous snakes in their services, claiming that it is within their religious right to do so.

EGG HEAD: The earth is flat! Pyramids were built by aliens! Birds aren't real! You might hear a public speaker spew some of these absurd theories, but if you live in Kentucky, there's nothing you can really do about it. According to one Kentucky law, "any person who interferes with any person addressing a public audience within this state, who interrupts such a person, while speaking, by the use of insulting or offensive language or opprobrious epithets applied to the speaker or who attempts to interrupt or injure the speaker by throwing missiles of any kind at him shall be fined not less than fifty ($50.00) nor more than five hundred dollars ($500), or imprisoned for not less than one (1) year nor more than six (6) months, or both." Thankfully, this law was repealed around 1975, so you are now free to fling whatever you like at the next conspiracy theorist who suggests something ridiculous, your dad included.

FISH AND ARROWS: If you want to go fishing in Kentucky, you're going to have to do it the old-fashioned way: in a boat with your grandpa and a flimsy wooden rod. That's because, in the Bluegrass State, it's illegal to use "nontraditional" methods of fishing. That means no underwater spears, no scuba diving, and, most importantly, no bow and arrows.

HIGHWAY CATWALK: It's June. You've been hitting the gym every day since January, trying to stay true to your New Year's resolution to lose weight and have the bikini body of your dreams. Now, it's time to debut your hard work. Where do you go? If you said, "the highway," then I have some very bad news. One obscure Kentucky law specifically forbids women between 99 and 199 pounds from walking along a highway in a bikini, unless escorted by a police officer. Weird? Lawmakers thought so too. This 1942 law was repealed in 1974.

BEE HAPPY, BEE HEALTHY: As the fifth most-obese state in the country, Kentucky doesn't hold its humans to the best health standard. Its bees, on the other hand . . . now that's another story. One Kentucky state law (that has since been repealed) required all bees entering the state to have certificates of health, stating that they are disease-free. You want to be a subpar bee? Go to South Carolina, why don't you?

LOUISIANA
N'awlins

SURPRISE FOOD: Your best friend's boyfriend just dumped her and you're halfway across the country doing something or other, and you need a way to cheer her up that doesn't involve dropping a fortune on a last-minute plane ticket to go comfort her. What about a surprise pizza?

Unfortunately, that won't work if you live in Louisiana. One law prevents the unauthorized ordering of goods or services. The law is especially concerned about those who place such orders as a prank, stating "it is unlawful for any person to intentionally place an order for any goods or services to be supplied or delivered to another person when . . . placing the order for goods or services intends to harass or annoy the person receiving such goods or services." Doing so can earn you a five-hundred-dollar dollar fine. So, stop trying to be a good person, ya hear?

CRAYFISH: Most people know crayfish (also known as *crawfish*) for one of two reasons: you either studied them in your middle school science class, or you ate them. Those from Louisiana are fond of the latter—the state has dubbed these lobster look-alikes "the official state crusta-cean" and have crafted dozens of Cajun dishes around the creature. Considering the animal's long history in the area, this comes as no surprise. Crayfish have been a staple of Louisiana culture for decades, ever since farmers realized that they could turn their flooded farms into crayfish plantations during the wet months. In the 1980s, when businesses figured out how to safely ship these crustaceans, they became a national delicacy, one that only Louisiana could properly provide.

All of this is to say, crayfish are deeply important to Louisianians. So important, in fact, that the state legislature drafted up a law stating that "whoever commits the crime of theft of crawfish . . . shall be imprisoned, with or without hard labor, for not more than ten years or may be fined not more than three thousand dollars, or both" (§ 14:67.5). That's a steep price to pay for a critter you can buy at Petco for less than the cost of a latte.

HAND IN HAND: What's that? You want to find out how deep your lifeline runs? Or if the indents near your thumb means that you'll come into money someday? Or why the notches by your wrist suddenly stop short? Well, you might have to take to the internet because palm readers—fortune-tellers that use the lines on your hand to determine whether or not you're going to have one child or thirteen—are banned in Louisiana. In fact, fortune-telling of any variety is illegal in the state, likely in response to tricksters trying to take advantage of drunken Mardi Gras crowds who, five drinks in, will drop two hundred dollars on a crystal ball reading without batting an eye.

BLOODY HELL: Louisiana is known for its food, its culture, and its voodoo. Originating from the traditions of the African diaspora, these beliefs were brought to the area through the slave trade centuries ago. However, while the practice itself is grounded more in spiritualism—baths, specialized diets, and prayers are common voodoo activities—many people associate the religion with dark magic traditions like blood sacrifices. Even the law upholds this misconception: Section 14:107.1 of the Louisiana revised statutes bans the ingesting of blood for the purposes of a ritual, claiming that the government is entitled to take whatever measures necessary "for the immediate preservation of the public peace, health, morals, safety, and welfare." The law also bans the mutilation of animals and the psychological manipulation of children for the same reasons.

TRUTH OR DARE: There's nothing more exciting than a good old-fashioned game of truth or dare. But is it even worth playing if you can't dare someone to go onto a railroad that you don't own? That's the question Louisianans must grapple with, thanks to one 1960 statute that forbids inciting, soliciting, urging, encouraging, exhorting, instigating, or procuring "any other person to go into or upon or to remain in or upon any structure, watercraft, or any other movable which belongs to another, including public buildings and structures, ferries, and bridges, or any part, portion, or area thereof, knowing that such other person has been forbidden to go or remain there, either orally or in writing, including by means of any sign hereinafter described, by the owner, lessee, or custodian of the property or by any other authorized person." Basically, if there's a sign forbidding it, and you dare someone to do it anyway, you're in big trouble.

MARYLAND
We've Got Crabs

WATCH YOUR MOUTH: Road rage may fly in other, less civilized states like Massachusetts (hear that, Massholes?) but not in Maryland. Rockville, Maryland—one town in this prim and proper East Coast state—has outlawed the use of profanity "upon or near any street, sidewalk or highway within the hearing of persons passing by, upon or along such street, sidewalk or highway" (laws of Rockville, Chapter. 12, § 12-1.00). Considered "disorderly behavior," swearing in public will result in a misdemeanor charge. That said, what qualifies as a curse word is still up for debate, so if you want to yell "malarkey" at an erratic driver or "monkeypaw" at a rowdy teenager, you're probably safe to do so.

LIONS, TIGERS, AND PROBABLY BEARS: Tired of domestic cats with names like Olaf and Bernie? Consider getting a tiger instead. They're bigger, stronger, and will definitely do a better job at defending you from intruders than your five-pound Calico. But wait: Did you say you lived in Maryland? In that case, never mind. On October 1, 2006, Maryland passed a law stating that it is illegal for individuals to "import, possess, breed or sell certain dangerous wild animals as pets in Maryland, including lions, tigers, servals, monkeys, wolves, wolf-dog hybrids, alligators and caimans." Animal sanctuaries and zoos are exempt, but your neighbor with the seven baboons in his backyard is not.

BIG BAD WOLF: If you live in Baltimore, Maryland, those chunky squirrels in your front yard may be more valuable than you think. Back in the 1600s, when the pilgrims packed their bags and made the journey out west, they brought with them more than just their religious beliefs— they unwittingly brought some of their political beliefs, too. As the New England colonies began to settle in and write their laws, they used some of their former masters' rules as guidelines for their own, including one set of laws called the Tudor Vermin Acts, which encouraged citizens to destroy "nuisance animals" to help preserve certain agricultural spaces. Maryland's version of these rules, which were laid out in a 1728 decree, encouraged citizens to destroy wolves, crows, and squirrels annually in exchange for tobacco or money. In fact, if you exceeded the required three scalps a year, you'd be granted additional bounty, and if you produced a full-on wolf head, you'd be granted a whopping two hundred pounds of tobacco. While it seems that this law is no longer in place, that hasn't stopped hunters from flinging bullets at poor, terrified squirrels in the forest all these years later.

TAKE THE LEAP: Most teenagers buy a scratch ticket or attend an R-rated movie when they hit eighteen. Maryland teens have a third option: jumping from a moving train. That's because, according to the Baltimore City Department of Legislative Reference, minors in the city of Baltimore are not allowed to leap from a railroad. The code was enacted in 1879, when the only activities to choose from were watching grass grow, kicking rocks, and, well, jumping off trains. But not to worry. If you're determined to fling yourself off of a railroad car before your eighteenth birthday, there is some good news: it's allowed so long as you work for the railroad company. So, apply now, before your youth escapes you.

BIRD BRAIN: Baltimore reveres their birds seriously. Within the city limits, it is illegal to "kill, injure, molest, or attempt to kill, injure, or molest, in any way, any bird" or "destroy, remove, or attempt to destroy or remove, any box placed in any tree or other suitable place in the City for the use of these birds" (city code, § 10-411). The code was enacted in 1976, thirteen years after the release of Alfred Hitchcock's *The Birds*, so we can only assume the increased interest in our avian friends triggered this move.

BYE-BYE BALLOON: Birthday parties in Baltimore, Maryland just aren't the same as the rest of the country. In February 2020, city lawmakers passed a bill that prohibits the intentional release of balloons, no matter the occasion. The bill was sponsored by environmental activists, who pointed out that rogue balloons have a terrible effect on wildlife and marine ecosystems, and is really just another, cuter form of littering. It's a shame, really. After all, how else are we supposed to mark the passage of time? If we don't wake up to a bundle of balloons in our bedroom, how will we know that we have inched another year closer to death?

MISSISSIPPI
It's All Fried

CHILD OF MINE: You've heard of blue laws—the premise for this entire book—but have you heard of love laws? These "adultery and fornication" rules have been around since the 1800s and, if enforced in their entirety, would result in some pretty packed prison systems. One law, for example, says that no unmarried couple can have intercourse. Ever. Even if they've been cohabitating for twenty years, and fight over bathroom products like married couples. Another law bans adultery in general.

However, the most fascinating law may be this one from Section 97-29-11 of the Mississippi code: "If any person, who shall have previously become the natural parent of an illegitimate child within or without this state by coition within or without this state, shall again become the natural parent of an illegitimate child born within this state, he or she shall be guilty of a misdemeanor and, upon conviction thereof, shall be punished by imprisonment in the county jail for not less than thirty (30) days nor more than ninety (90) days or by a fine of not more than Two Hundred Fifty Dollars ($ 250.00), or both." Translation? You cannot have more than one illegitimate child in the state of Mississippi. One out-of-wedlock kid? Fine. We all make mistakes. But two? Get your wallet. You're about to pay your dues.

HOW DISTURBING: It's happening. You've finally decided that you're going to confess your feelings to your crush. One problem. They're currently in church. If you live anywhere else in the country, you're well within your right to burst into the service and proclaim your love for all to hear. But if you live in the state of Mississippi, you're going to have to wait until the service is over. That's because Section 97-35-17 of the Mississippi code states, "if any person shall willfully disturb any congregation of persons lawfully assembled for religious worship, he may be immediately arrested by any officer or private person, without warrant, and taken before any justice court judge of the county, present or convenient, and on conviction thereof by such justice, municipal, county or circuit court, shall be fined not more than Five Hundred Dollars ($500.00) or imprisoned not more than six (6) months, or both." Mississippians take their worship seriously, and you need to respect that, or else.

DEAD MEAT: By now, we are all aware of the dangers of eating obscure animals—bat meat was the very source of COVID-19, the pandemic that has made us all shudder at the words *social distancing* and *quarantine*. But Mississippi was way ahead of the game. A state law dating back to 1892 prevents the sale of consumption of "unclean" animals, including cats and dogs. More specifically, it says that "if any person shall sell or offer for sale as human food, the flesh of any animal which shall have died a natural death, or been killed or injured by any accident; or shall sell, or offer for sale, or ship for sale, as human food, the flesh of any diseased animal, or of any dog, cat, or other like unclean animal, such person shall be fined, on conviction, not less than one hundred dollars and imprisoned not less than thirty days." So, Mr. Dog can rest safe at night knowing that you have no plans to eat him in his sleep.

LOVE IS LOVE: You can teach your kids that love is only between a man and a woman, or a man and a man, or a woman and a woman, or a dog and a frog, but you cannot under any circumstances teach them that love is between a man, a woman, and another woman, or another man, or any combination of the three. The teaching of polygamy is banned in the state under Section 97-29-43 of the Mississippi code, which says that "if any person shall teach another the doctrines, principles, or tenets, or any of them, of polygamy; or shall endeavor so to do; or shall induce or persuade another by words or acts, or otherwise, to embrace or adopt polygamy, or to emigrate to any other state, territory, district, or country for the purpose of embracing, adopting, or practicing polygamy, or shall endeavor so to do, he shall, on conviction, be fined not less than twenty-five dollars nor more than five hundred dollars, or be imprisoned in the county jail not less than one month nor more than six months, or both." What's interesting is that this law does not ban the act of polygamy itself—just the teaching of it. So, Mississippians are free to marry whoever they want and however many people they want, as long as they don't go off and brag about it.

HOME-FREE: There's more than one way to become homeless. Maybe you lose your job, and you can't afford your mortgage. Maybe your house burns down, and you forgot to get that specific type of insurance, leaving you penniless. Maybe you are an aspiring actor who can't afford an apartment and chooses instead to live in their car. Whatever the reason, the outcome is the same if you live in Mississippi: a large fine and likely jail time. In this southern state, homelessness is punishable by law. One statute defines "every able-bodied person who lives without employment or labor, and who has no visible means of support" as vagrants and promises to "commit the person to jail for not less than ten nor more than thirty days, or shall require such person to give bond." Talk about adding insult to injury.

IT'S GOOD FOR YOU: As of 2020, Mississippi had the highest rate of obesity in the United States. Rather than help curb this problem, the state had another idea: what if they eliminated nutrition label requirements and allowed restaurants to blindly serve foods with extraordinary calorie counts? In 2013, the state passed a law waiving the need to include nutrition labels in restaurants. Phil Bryant, the governor responsible for the law, argued that "it is simply not the role of government to micro-regulate citizens' dietary decisions."

NORTH CAROLINA
Just Beachy

BINGO: What has five letters and strict restrictions in the state of North Carolina? Bingo! No, really. It's bingo. Not only is this simple game heavily restricted in North Carolina (for example, you cannot play a game of bingo for longer than five hours), but also it is not allowed to be played drunk. Per the 2015 North Carolina general statutes, "it shall be unlawful to sell or consume, or for the owner or other person in charge of the premises to allow the sale or consumption of, any alcoholic beverage in any room while a raffle or bingo game is being conducted in that room." No more drinks for Grandma.

COSTUME PARTY: Now, everybody knows office jobs are not the most thrilling. No. matter how many swear jars or beer carts companies roll out, they'll never be able to spice up the nine-to-five slog that

Dolly Parton once wrote about. Not even costume parties can liven up corporate life, and, even if they could, they wouldn't be allowed anyway. The North Carolina General Assembly states that "no person or persons at least sixteen years of age shall while wearing a mask, hood or device whereby the person, face or voice is disguised so as to conceal the identity of the wearer, hold any manner of meeting, or make any demonstration upon the private property of another" (§ 14-12.10). Meaning, you can't wear a costume to a meeting, or anything that disguises your voice or face. Stick with the blazer. It looks nice.

TRUCKIN' IT: Your sixteen-wheeler truck road trip may need to wait until Monday. In the state of North Carolina (and, in fact, in most states), it is illegal to drive oversize vehicles on Sundays. The North Carolina Department of Transportation's shipping regulations allow travel between "sunrise to sunset Monday through Saturday with no travel allowed on Sunday. Continuous travel is permitted if heavy only and under 112,000 pounds." It's unclear exactly why such laws exist, other than to force workaholic drivers to take a break every once in a while.

PINING FOR NEEDLES: If a Brit were to come to the United States, they might assume that every state is pretty much the same, but the truth is, every area of this country is wildly different with a variety of specialties. California, for example, is known for its wine. Idaho is synonymous with potatoes. And North Carolina has, apparently, pine straw. Out of the sixty available species of pine, North Carolina has eight of them within its borders. That's a lot of pine. So much pine, in fact, that the state's residents have desperately started to look for ways to get rid of it. Luckily, they found one. As it turns out, pine straws are a good alternative to mulch—they prevent water from evaporating from the soil and can weigh down nasty weeds. For this reason, North Carolinians have started collecting pine needles and selling them to landscapers across the country to turn a profit.

While this unlikely business has made North Carolina a secret gem in the landscaping world, it has also forged divides between its residents, who, upon realizing the power of the straw, began to fight over the commodity. That's why in 1997, a law was put in place forbidding residents from stealing their neighbors' pine needles. The law states that "If any person shall take and carry away, or shall aid in taking or carrying away, any pine needles or pine straw being produced on the land of another person . . . with the intent to steal the pine needles or pine straw, that person shall be guilty of a Class H felony" (§ 14-79.1). If you want that pine needle money, you're going to have to put in that pine needle work.

COOPED UP: Chicken on the loose? You better hope not. In Ahoskie, North Carolina, it is illegal for chickens or other fowl to roam freely or "be at large," a phrase which, frankly, makes it sound like there's a group of criminal chickens on the run in Ahoskie. Did you know that chickens could rob banks? Me either. The town also has laws against owning loud roosters or generally annoying animals, so leave your parrots and chihuahuas back in Brooklyn, or whatever overpriced city you'll be moving from.

SOUTH CAROLINA
Palmetto Paradise

DEADLOOSE: Was Elvis Presley really sent by the devil to poison the souls of our children with his dance moves? It's hard to say. But just to be safe, the state of South Carolina took some preventative measures—in 1962, they drafted a law banning dance halls from operating too closely to churches or cemeteries (Section 52-13-10). Though the rule was likely created to prevent churchgoers from being seduced away from the chapel by blasting music, the reason for including "cemeteries" in the text is unclear. Do they know something we don't? Can music raise the dead somehow? Is that why Jesus rose on the third day? Did he hear some rockin' hymns and decide to join in?

CIRCUS ACT: In South Carolina, circuses are totally allowed, so long as they only stick around for less than forty-eight hours. Anything longer than that and they'll get in trouble with the law, which states that "circuses shall not be licensed for a time exceeding forty-eight hours at one place in any one year" (South Carolina code § 52-1-30). Why? According to the animal advocacy groups that pushed for these restrictions, forcing elephants, monkeys, and the like to perform multiple days in a row is dangerous and abusive. Who knew?

BORED GAMES: Want to host a game night? Then pack your bags and drive to the next state over, because South Carolina won't allow it: the state has prohibited any game that uses cards or dice. The law came to light in 2007 when one group of citizens tried to host a charity poker event and were swiftly shut down thanks to this lesser-known ruling. Despite their complaints, lawmakers refused to take the law off the books even though they themselves admitted that it's not always enforceable. After all, there are dozens of dangerous eight-year-olds out there, hiding in the shadows of seedy South Carolinian suburbs, just waiting for parents to go to bed so they can gamble away their paper bills on ritzy Monopoly properties. How irresponsible.

MARRY ME: These days, you'd be hard-pressed to find a man who chooses marriage; most are bullied into it by passive-aggressive mothers-in-law or swayed by the promise of tax breaks. But these unicorn men must have existed at some point in America's history, because in 1963, South Carolina passed a law (which has since been repealed) prohibiting men from seducing unmarried women using deception or promises of getting hitched. Section 16-15-50 of the South Carolina code of laws states that "a male over the age of sixteen years who by means of deception and promise of marriage seduces an unmarried woman in this State is guilty of a misdemeanor." It also specifies, however, that "there must not be a conviction under this section on the uncorroborated testimony of the woman upon whom the seduction is charged, and no conviction if at trial it is proved that the woman was at the time of the alleged offense lewd and unchaste." So, if the woman in question had no witnesses to the seduction, she's obviously lying, right? That's how the law works? Pics or it didn't happen?

PINBALL PLEASE: Cigarettes? Totally innocent. Violent video games? Not destructive at all. But pinball? That's the devil's machine. Or so it goes in the state of South Carolina where individuals under the age of eighteen were long barred from playing this arcade favorite. Apparently, lawmakers considered pinball dangerously similar to gambling and wanted to prevent unsuspecting youths from dropping their allowance on these bells-and-whistles boxes every weekend. Thankfully, the state came to its senses and repealed the law around 2016.

TENNESSEE
The Home of Honky Tonk

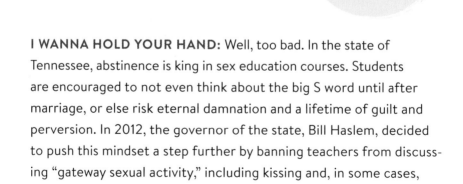

I WANNA HOLD YOUR HAND: Well, too bad. In the state of Tennessee, abstinence is king in sex education courses. Students are encouraged to not even think about the big S word until after marriage, or else risk eternal damnation and a lifetime of guilt and perversion. In 2012, the governor of the state, Bill Haslem, decided to push this mindset a step further by banning teachers from discussing "gateway sexual activity," including kissing and, in some cases, hand-holding. The bill passed with a whopping sixty-eight votes (only twenty-three voted against it), leaving teenagers in the state wondering what is even left to do with their partners. Hugging? Cuddling? Long, uninterrupted stares?

GOVERNOR DUEL: Every politician has dirty laundry: a secret affair, an illegitimate child, a picture of them smoking weed in college. Most of these things are fair game and won't ruin a person's career. In Kentucky, though, there's one exception. If you are running for public office, you cannot have ever been in a duel. Even a fake one. Even a real one. Even one involving cardboard tubes stolen from Christmas wrapping paper conducted in your backyard under the watchful eye of your grandmother. Give up your dreams.

STREAMING WARS: In the early 2000s, pirating music was so easy, children were doing it in their spare time using sites like Limewire, to the annoyance of musicians everywhere. Over the years, the problem didn't disappear; it simply mutated. Now, instead of Limewire, there's Spotify—a music service with a virtually unlimited library that you can share with your family and friends. The television and movie industry has joined in on the fun, too, launching services like Netflix and Hulu that allow users to share their passwords willy-nilly. While some states in the United States have allowed this practice to continue, others like Tennessee have lost their patience. That's why in 2011, after severe pressure from lobbyists to curb illegal streaming and shared accounts, Governor Bill Haslem passed a law criminalizing shared log-ins on entertainment subscription services.

BOOB TUBE: Hollywood would have you believe that every strip club in the country is filled with topless women holding trays of alcohol and trying to seduce horny men, but that's not entirely true. In the state of Tennessee, exposed breasts are actually prohibited at any establishment that serves alcohol. The rule states that it is unlawful "to employ, use or allow any person in the sale or service of alcoholic beverages or malt beverages in or upon the licensed premises while such person is unclothed or in such attire, costume or clothing as to expose to view any portion of the female breast below the top of the areola or of any portion of the pubic hair, anus, cleft of the buttocks, vulva or genitals." So, if you're trying to get a little something-something, maybe consider one of the other forty-nine states.

SOMETHING STINKS: Do you smell that? It smells like a criminal to me. According to Tennessee code annotated law 70-4-208, "it is unlawful for any person to import, possess, or cause to be imported into this state any type of live skunk, or to sell, barter, exchange or other-wise transfer any live skunk." Anyone who does will have their skunks confiscated and euthanized. What is it about skunks that Southerners hate so much? Is it their stench? Their tails? Their stubby little legs that force them to wobble back and forth like like constipated penguins? Has anyone asked?

VIRGINIA
Sweeter Than Sweet Tea

RAT BANDITS: Raccoons have a bad rap. Sure, they may dig through trash cans, ripping the plastic bag to shreds and leaving discarded junk all over your driveway and yeah, they might occasionally have rabies, but does that make them worthy of such negative treatment? Virginia seems to think so. Embedded in the hunting and trapping section of the state code is a law stating that it is illegal to kill any and all animals on Sundays . . . except for raccoons. Those are totally fair game.

TAXI ESCORT: Taxis are a little bit like Vegas: what happens inside a cab, stays inside a cab. Which is to say, drivers for car services hear a lot of insane stories: roommate drama, family affairs, the occasional murder confession, etc. For the most part, they keep this information to themselves. In the state of Virginia, there is one exception: car service drivers cannot transport a passenger who is on their way to engage in illicit sexual behavior.

The rule states that "it is unlawful for any person or any officer, employee, or agent of any firm, association, or corporation with knowledge of, or good reason to believe, the immoral purpose of such visit, to take or transport or assist in taking or transporting, or offer to take or transport on foot or in any way, any person to a place, whether within or outside any building or structure, used or to be used for the purpose of lewdness, assignation, or prostitution within the Commonwealth or to procure or assist in procuring for the purpose of illicit sexual intercourse" (§ 18.2-348). While this law seems to have been made to discourage prostitution, the vague language allows for a broader interpretation, one that puts taxi drivers who overhear their passenger gushing about booty calls in hot water.

CAR SEX: In the same breath that Virginia outlawed transporting sexual deviants (see the Taxi Escort entry in this section), they also outlawed another beloved activity: car sex. Section 18.2-349 of the Virginia state code says that "it is unlawful for any owner or chauffeur of any vehicle, with knowledge or reason to believe the same is to be used for such purpose, to use the same or to allow the same to be used for the purpose of prostitution or unlawful sexual intercourse or to aid or promote such prostitution or unlawful sexual intercourse by the use of any such vehicle. A violation of this section is a Class 1 misdemeanor. However, any adult who violates this section by using a vehicle or allowing a vehicle to be used for or to aid or promote prostitution or unlawful sexual intercourse with a person under the age of eighteen is guilty of a Class 6 felony." Of course, some of the phrasing here leaves this law open to interpretation. After all, what is considered "unlawful" sexual intercourse? Two teenagers running off to have some alone time in their parents' minivan? A science teacher sneaking away to have an affair with the math teacher? Your parents getting it on in the driveway in an attempt to rekindle the spark? Up to you.

DIRTY BOOKS: The children are our future. We must keep them safe and shield them from any negative influences. Virginia has taken the first step toward doing just that by banning "obscene books." According to one Virginia Beach law, any person who believes a book is too dirty for distribution can bring their case before the court. If the court agrees, that book can be banned in certain areas. What makes this law tricky is that the definition of "obscene" can vary from person to person. So, while one mother may think Harry Potter is a heartwarming tale of friendship and magic, another may view it as a gateway to voodoo, witchcraft, and, like, communism or something.

TRICK OR TREAT: How old is too old to trick or treat? Is it when the child realizes that they don't have to take "just one" of the treats from the unguarded candy bowl? Is it when the child's voice drops from puberty and starts scaring away all the other trick-or-treaters? Or is

it when the trick-or-treater reaches the same height as the person answering the door? In most places, the question is still up for debate, but not Virginia. Across the state, cities have started implementing age limits on trick-or-treaters. In Chesapeake Bay, that limit is fourteen, meaning anyone who can officially be called a teenager must find another activity to engage in on October 31.

WEST VIRGINIA
West Virginia, Best Virginia

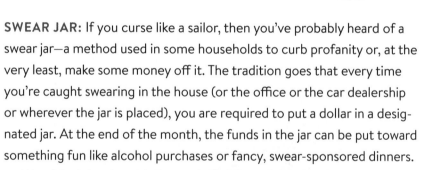

SWEAR JAR: If you curse like a sailor, then you've probably heard of a swear jar—a method used in some households to curb profanity or, at the very least, make some money off it. The tradition goes that every time you're caught swearing in the house (or the office or the car dealership or wherever the jar is placed), you are required to put a dollar in a designated jar. At the end of the month, the funds in the jar can be put toward something fun like alcohol purchases or fancy, swear-sponsored dinners.

West Virginia takes this "swear jar" philosophy seriously, so much so that it has implemented a statewide ruling punishing anyone who profanely curses in public. The penalty? One dollar for every offense. While the law, recorded in 2005, seems to no longer be on the books, the people want to know: What happened to the money? Did we spend it on a six-pack? A lottery ticket? The offenders are usually in the loop about things like this.

RED FLAGS: West Virginia is wary of red flags—metaphorically and literally. Per one West Virginia law that has been around since at least 2005, it is illegal to display "any red or black flag, or to display any other flag, emblem, device or sign of any nature whatever, indicating sympathy with or support of ideals, institutions or forms of government, hostile, inimical or antagonistic to the form or spirit of the constitution, laws, ideals and institutions of this state or of the United States." What makes a red flag so abhorrent? Well, red flags have long been associated with left-wing politics: there is an age-old association between socialism/communism and the color red, thanks to the handful of socialist and communist countries that use the color in their national flags. There is even a socialist anthem titled, quite literally, "The Red Flag." So, it's no surprise, then, that a country like America, which boasts a long and complicated history with such political parties, would reject any symbol associated with them.

HATS OFF TO WEST VIRGINIA: If Abraham Lincoln were alive today and in desperate need of a movie night, he would have to make a few compromises. One law dating back to 2005 states that "no person attending any performance at any theater, hall or opera house, or any such building where theatrical or other performances are given, when an admission fee is charged, shall wear upon his or her head any hat, bonnet or covering for the head which may obstruct the view of any person or persons during the performance." Anyone guilty of ruining someone else's viewing experience in this way will be hit with a misdemeanor charge and a ten-dollar fine. So, if Abe wants to see the latest *Avengers*, he's going to have to lose the hat, or else cough up a few bucks.

KILLIN' IT: To West Virginians, "one person's trash is another person's treasure" applies to everything, even the carcass sitting on the side of the road. That's because, in this state, it is totally legal to scrape a dead animal off the pavement and bring it home for dinner, per state code §20-2-4. Proponents of the "roadkill law" claim that it saves the state money by sparing highway workers from having to waste hours scouring the streets for dead animals. They also point to the various traditions that have sprung up around the bill, including the town of Marlinton's annual roadkill festival, in which visitors compete to produce the most interesting roadkill dish. Past examples include turtle gumbo, bear meat chili, and alligator stew.

LEWD COHABITATION: Kissing? No. Sex? Absolutely not. Cuddles? Get out of here. If you live with someone in the state of West Virginia and you try to do any of these things, you're in deep trouble. According to one 1931 law, "if any persons, not married to each other, lewdly and lasciviously associate and cohabit together, or, whether married or not, be guilty of open or gross lewdness and lasciviousness, they shall be guilty of a misdemeanor, and, upon conviction, shall be fined not less than fifty dollars, and may, in the discretion of the court, be imprisoned not exceeding six months, and, upon a repetition of the offense, they shall, upon conviction, be confined in jail not less than six nor more than twelve months." In other words, if you want to do anything that the state might consider "lewd," you better put a ring on it.

THE SOUTHWEST

Cowboy Country

When Southerners say, "go big or go home," they mean it. Though it may only amount to four states (Oklahoma, Texas, New Mexico, Arizona), the Southwest is larger in size than all of the Northeast combined, and larger in personality. Home to cowboys, national parks, and charming accents, the Southwest offers visitors a picturesque American experience. It also offers a picturesque religious experience, as the only thing bigger than a Southerner's heart is their Bible. With two states (Texas and Oklahoma) in the Bible Belt and two (Arizona and New Mexico) in the Sun belt, the Southwest splits their time between loving Jesus and loving the sun. And who can blame them?

ARIZONA
Truly Grand

DAZED AND CONFUSED: A popular high school prank involves taking a plastic baggie, filling it with herbs, and peddling it to young, gullible freshmen looking to buy weed. By the time they figure out their mistake (perhaps after their third or fourth painful puff of burnt rosemary), you'll be ankles deep in candy or coffee or whatever you choose to use your winnings on. This clever stint might fly in most states, but not in Arizona. Section 13-3451 of the Arizona revised statutes outlines some of the state's laws against illegal substances, including manufacturing imitation drugs. In other words, not only are you prohibited from making real drugs, but you're also prohibited from making fake drugs. Basically, if it starts with *D* and ends in *RUGS*, it's off-limits.

GARBAGE PIG: Before you say that pigs are living garbage disposals that will consume anything you throw at them, consider this: human beings have, on average, around 9,000 taste buds. Pigs have around 15,000. It makes sense, then, that Arizona would impose a rule forbidding anyone from feeding garbage to swine—if you wouldn't feed it to a person, you shouldn't feed it to a pig. The rule, however, has one exception: "No person shall feed garbage to swine without first obtaining a permit from the associate director. All permits shall be renewed during January of each year." So, if farmers are determined to empty their trash cans into their pig pens, they can request a permit to do so in order to bypass this law. Literal trash has never tasted so sweet.

BIRD BRAIN: Before you shoot that hawk out of the sky in Arizona, think long and hard about what exactly you're going to do with it, because if you're not planning on eating every single morsel, you could be subjected to some gnarly fines. According to Section 17-309 of Arizona's fish and game laws, it's illegal to "take a game bird, game mammal or game fish and knowingly permit an edible portion thereof to go to waste." This leaves some big questions to consider, like: How are you going to cook the beak? Boil it? Fry it? Stick it in the microwave? What about the toenails? The feathers? If you can't handle the responsibility of eating a bird in full, maybe you shouldn't be allowed to kill it in the first place. Just a thought.

CACTUS CATCH: You might think of a cactus as "that spiky plant you see in desert photographs," but there is so much more to them than their prickly exteriors. Saguaro cacti are particularly special. These plants can only be found in the Sonoran Desert—a chunk of land stretching from Baja, California, to the corner of Arizona—and can weigh four tons when fully hydrated. Not only that, but these thirsty guys can take almost eight years to grow a single inch. This fact in particular makes preserving them that much more important. (After all, imagine how you'd feel if it took your child 520 years to reach a normal size, only to have them killed? It would be traumatic, for so many reasons.) This is why there is law in the Grand Canyon State that forbids anyone from moving a cactus, period. Native plants are protected and should be left alone, like the feral cat in your backyard or your girlfriend after you've done something stupid to annoy her.

THERE'S A CATCH: If you've ever dropped twenty dollars on one of those arcade crane games in hopes of winning a stuffed bear or an iPhone, only to walk away empty-handed, then you've probably had a thought along the lines of "Man, that game is totally rigged." If you live anywhere outside of Arizona, you're probably right, but if you live within this arid state, then you're probably just bad at the game because according to one state law, "altering or maintaining a crane game so that the claw is physically unable to grasp exposed prizes" is illegal.

DONKEY TUB: Is it illegal for a donkey to sleep in a bathtub in Arizona? The story goes that in 1924, a donkey was spotted floating down a flooded river in a bathtub, sparking widespread confusion. After some questioning, officials determined that the donkey's owner had carelessly left a tub outside of their house, which the donkey promptly stepped into and fell asleep before being washed away by floodwaters. The amount of money and energy spent trying to rescue the donkey convinced the citizens of the town to create a law banning donkeys from sleeping in bathtubs.

The only problem? The story's not true. This myth has been floating around the internet for a few years and has even been picked up by a few lawyer blogs despite the fact that it has been thoroughly debunked.

NEW MEXICO
Hot and Spicy

DUMB LAW: The 2016 US election was momentous for two totally unrelated reasons. First, Donald Trump won the US presidential race, returning the White House back to Republicans, and second, "idiots" were officially granted the right to vote in New Mexico. Since its founding, the state has changed its voting laws dozens of times, proving itself as one of the more indecisive corners of the country. In one of those decisions back in 1967, the lawmakers of New Mexico declared that "every citizen of the United States who is over the age of twenty-one years and has resided in New Mexico twelve months, in the county ninety days, and in the precinct in which he the person offers to vote thirty days, next preceding the election, except idiots, insane persons, and person convicted of a felonious or infamous crime unless restored to political rights, shall be qualified to vote at all elections." In the context of the 1960s, the word *idiot* here refers to those with mental illness or disability, which is not funny at all. What is funny is that this law was still on the books until 2016—long after the word's terrible ableist association. These days, the word "idiot" just means "a plain ol' dummy," making this age-old rule plainly laughable.

"O FAIR NEW MEXICO": State pride is part of what makes living in America so great. (Where else can you fight to the death over baseball teams or debate the subtleties of local accents for hours?) Fortunately, New Mexico has a lot of pride. In fact, the Land of the Midnight Sun (which is, perhaps, the best state nickname) has so much pride that they have deemed misusing the state anthem a literal crime. Section 30-21-5 of their state code prohibits the "improper use of official anthems" which "consists of singing, playing or rendering 'The Star-Spangled Banner' or 'Oh Fair New Mexico' in any public place or assemblage in this state except as an entire or separate composition or number." A trash state like Texas might let that fly but in this pseudo-desert, we sing songs right. (No offense, Texas. That's the state pride talking again.)

THROW THE GAME: New Mexico loves its sports as much as the next guy, but it may be one of the only places that has criminalized interfering with them. According to one statute, interference with an athletic event by way of "intentionally throwing any object on or across the field of play . . . with the intent to interfere with the normal conduct of that event while the contestants of that event are on that field" is a big no-no that will result in a petty misdemeanor and a crowd of angry fans with pitchforks chasing you down the road. Throwing that frisbee onto the football field to stir confusion is just not worth it, no matter how funny.

EQUINE EQUITY: There is a law in New Mexico that forbids the "unlawful tripping of an equine . . . for the purpose of sport or entertainment." What did horses do to be treated with such disrespect in the first place? How many times do they have to carry humans around scenic countrysides for forty bucks a pop, making them feel downright majestic, before we'll consider not tripping them for our own enjoyment? How many jousting tournaments and cinematic battles do they have to endure before we'll give them a break? Will they ever be able to roam green pastures, chomping on grass and bathing in the sun, without fear of being interrupted by some sniffling, attention-seeking human? The equine world demands answers.

FIVE-STAR SERVICE: How do you know when your waiter is bad at their job? When they mess up every single one of your orders? When they spill your food all over your lap by accident or perhaps "by accident"? When they end their shift and forget to tell their boss, abandoning you at the restaurant until someone notices that you have been sitting around sipping your lukewarm water for an hour? All of these things are probably true but, in New Mexico, you're going to have to work harder if you want to be considered an "indecent waiter." In this state, "indecent waitering" is illegal and defined as "a person [who] knowingly and intentionally [exposes] his intimate parts to public view while serving beverage or food in a licensed liquor establishment. 'Intimate parts' means the mons pubis, penis, testicles, mons veneris, vulva, female breast, or vagina. As used in this section, 'female breast' means the areola and 'exposing' does not include any act in which the intimate part is covered by any nontransparent material."

GLUED TO THE PAGE: If you didn't slather your fingers in glue as a child and peel off its dried remnants like snakeskin, then you missed out on one of the world's greatest joys. I'm talking to you, Carlsbad, New Mexico. In this southern town, you cannot give glue to a minor (read: anyone under eighteen) without a parent's consent. That means seventeen-year-olds may be able to see R-rated movies and drive cars, but they can't embark on any arts and crafts projects without getting permission from their mom or dad.

OKLAHOMA
It's Nothing Like the Musical

HOT GOSS: It's unclear how nosy mothers are able to survive in Oklahoma, considering this state's law against eavesdropping. Buried deep within the state's records, there is a statute from 1910 that says, "every person guilty of secretly loitering about any building, with intent to overhear discourse therein, and to repeat or publish the same to vex, annoy, or injure others, is guilty of a misdemeanor." That means all spies, meddling parents, and gossipy popular girls will suffer the same fate if they sneak around, waiting to overhear something juicy or incriminating.

SMELLY AND STICKY: Is there a shortage of glue in the southwest? Did some three-year-old ingest some Elmer's in arts class and get the sticky substance banned, forcing Oklahoma residents to seek out another adhesive? It's the only explanation we can think of for this Tulsa rule, which forbids the business of "making glue from any part of dead animals, drying, storing any blood, scrap, fat, grease, dried skunk hides or green skunk hides, or the conducting of any business or occupation that will or does generate any unwholesome, offensive or deleterious odors, gas, smoke, or exhalation, or that is or would be dangerous or detrimental to life or health, shall be carried on anywhere in the City of Tulsa without a permit from the Director of Health." Keep your smelly crafts to yourself.

GET IN, WHORE: Catcalling is a major problem for American women. That's why, in 1910, Oklahoma put their foot down, implementing a law that prohibited anyone from calling women whores, or any other name that would imply a "want of chastity." The law goes: "If any person shall orally or otherwise, falsely and maliciously or falsely and wantonly impute to any female, married or unmarried, a want of chastity, he shall be deemed guilty of slander, and upon conviction shall be fined not less than Twenty-five Dollars ($25.00) nor more than Five Hundred Dollars ($500.00), or by imprisonment in the county jail not less than thirty (30) days nor more than ninety (90) days, or by both such fine and imprisonment." Unfortunately, in 2017, this law, along with many other "antiquated" laws, were repealed by the state in an effort to update the its criminal code. Arguing that such a law is "antiquated" feels strange—ask any woman if they've been called an unsavory name recently for not responding to a man's advances, and you'll get dozens of stories—but hey, we're not the experts.

MAY GOD HAVE MERCY: In church, you worship. That's it. You don't walk to the front of the room and announce a surprise wedding service, nor do you profess your love for your sister's husband in front of her entire family, and you certainly don't cause an uproar mid-prayer by saying something inflammatory like "God isn't real" or "I think my dad's an alien." Oklahoma knows this well. In fact, the state implemented a rule in 1910 that prevents anyone from willfully disturbing, interrupting, or disquieting "any assemblage of people met for religious worship." Doing so will earn you a misdemeanor and a very nasty look from your pastor, so it might be best to just save it for after the service, yeah?

LOOK HERE: You would never touch a stranger's walking cane, right? Or push the buttons on some ailing senior citizen's oxygen machine? Or rip out your grandpa's hearing aid? So why, then, would you touch somebody's glasses without their permission? The answer is you wouldn't. Or, rather, you shouldn't, as it would impede their ability to function. Oklahoma doesn't trust people to follow this basic rule of decency, though, which is why they have created a law to limit the unlawful touching of glasses and other assistive devices. It states that "every person who, without justifiable or excusable cause and with intent to harass, touches any assistive device of another person, shall upon conviction, be guilty of a misdemeanor punishable by imprisonment in the county jail for a period of not more than one (1) year, or by a fine not to exceed One Thousand Dollars ($1,000.00), or by both such fine and imprisonment." As they say in grade school: you can look, but you can't touch.

TEXAS
Go Big or Go Home

BELIEVE ME, I KNOW: In Texas, you can believe in whatever you want. God, Satan, a generic Supreme Being, a sentient toy car—you name it. The only thing off-limits is not believing in anything, at least if you're planning on running for public office. According to the 11th Biennial Report of the State of Texas, published in 1898, "No religious test shall ever be required as a qualification to any office or public trust in this State; nor shall anyone be excluded from holding office on account of his religious sentiments, provided he acknowledges the existence of a Supreme Being." Now, you might be thinking, "Yes, but this law was published in the 19th century—of course it's going to be a little wacky and antiquated!" But here's the twist: this line remains in the Texas constitution to this day. Many politicians and concerned citizens have challenged the ruling over the years, hoping to strike the problematic last line and pave the way for an atheist leader, but to no avail.

EYE SPY: We all make jokes about selling our organs on the black market to make a quick buck and pay off some shady loans, but no one actually does it, right? Right? Wrong. Organ trafficking is, unfortunately, a modern problem. While most countries have banned the practice outright, some, like Iran, have yet to officially denounce it, opening up dangerous opportunities for illegal organ harvesting. This is why it's not totally unsurprising that Texas has a rule in their penal code prohibiting activities related to this, like selling your own eye. Despite the preexisting federal prohibition of organ trafficking, the state of Texas decided to seek extra protection against these behaviors and set aside a whole section of their legislature to address the problem. In "Prohibition of the Purchase and Sale of Human Organs," it states that it's illegal to trade any of the following: human kidney, liver, heart, lung, pancreas, eye, bone, skin, or any other human organ or tissue. Hair is not included.

THEY DO: It's Monday, the morning of your wedding, and you slept through your alarm. In a panic, you grab your tux, your something borrowed, and your car keys, only to realize that it's too late—the traffic on the 405 is backed up for miles and there's no way you'll make it in time. What do you do? Easy. Ask a friend to do it for you. In the state of Texas, marriage by proxy is fully legal. Though originally created around 1997 to help incarcerated fiancés marry their partners, the law was adjusted in 2013—it now only applies to active military and "those unable to attend," which seems dangerously vague.

REMEMBER THE ALAMO: You've heard of the saying "don't forget the Alamo," but what about "don't pee on the Alamo"? Well, it exists, and it was brought starkly to light in 2014 when a young El Paso resident whizzed on the monument in a drunken stupor and earned himself a felony charge for "Criminal Mischief of a Public Monument or Place of Human Burial." Believe it or not, though, that's not even the most famous tale. Rumor has it that Black Sabbath singer Ozzy Osbourne once peed on the famous statue in 1992, though he and his bandmates claim it was actually the building across the street. Nonetheless, the artist paid a hefty charity donation to show his regret, while the El Paso offender paid $4,000 in damages. It pays to get peed on, apparently.

NOT YOUR COW: There are plenty of cows to go around in Texas, so it seems silly to even suggest that milking a stranger's cow was once a problem, but alas, it's true. Since at least 1866, there has been a law in the state of Texas preventing anyone from milking someone else's cow: "Whoever without the consent of the owner shall take up, use or milk any cow, not his own, shall be fined not exceeding ten dollars." Unfortunately for the cows, it was repealed in 1973.

THE WEST
Hipsters and Hollywood

Californians may have you believe that the only thing worth seeing out West is the Hollywood sign, but the other ten states (Washington, Montana, Idaho, Oregon, Wyoming, Colorado, Utah, Nevada, Alaska, and Hawaii) might disagree. From Seattle's booming coffee culture to Portland's robust hipster population to Las Vegas's sleepless nights, there's plenty to do outside of the Golden State. Don't get us wrong—California, which admittedly takes up a large portion of the West's real estate—has its perks, including jealousy-inducing weather, movie stars, and quality Mexican food, but there's more to this region than just wine and avocados. On any given day in the Western United States, you can find people sipping cocktails from coconuts, mingling with Mormons, trudging through snow, or farming potatoes—whatever suits your fancy. So, pack up your things, leave your worries behind, and head out to the final frontier! But maybe set aside some extra time—traffic gets bad this time of year.

ALASKA
Every Season Is Hunting Season

DON'T BE WASTEFUL: Wasting meat in Alaska is not just a crime, it's a sign of disrespect: for the community, for fellow hunters, and for the animals themselves. Hunting is a regulated, and in some cases necessary, sport, so it's important to follow the rules and honor the traditions of the area you're hunting in. For example: in some areas of Alaska, excess meat is passed along to villagers. But when the hunters are inexperienced or don't follow the law, and show up with stacks of spoiled meat, it can anger communities who rely on hunting communities for their food supply or other valuable goods made from the animal carcasses.

That's why in Alaska, it has been deemed illegal to "waste" any part of a big game animal, including, most notably, a moose. Listed in Alaska's 31st legislature is a code demanding that "a person taking game shall salvage the following parts for human use . . . the head, heart, liver, kidneys, stomach and hide of moose . . . and all edible meat" for "human consumption." On top of that, all aforementioned meat "of the front quarters and hindquarters must remain naturally attached to the bone until the meat is transported from the field or is processed for human consumption." Not only can you be charged upward of ten thousand dollars by refusing to do so, but you may also end up burning bridges in the community, which is something you don't want to do in a place this small. (Alaska is the fourth least populated state in the United States. So, if you screw up, everyone will know. Just like high school!)

TAKE A WALK: There are plenty of strange stories about people who have domesticated moose, but perhaps the best one comes out of Fairbanks where, in 1913, a bartender named Pete Buckholtz acquired a calf from a group of hunters and began raising it as his own. Pete and the moose became inseparable, to the point where the moose began following Pete into the saloon where he worked. While there, Pete would occasionally slip the creature alcohol, turning a bad situation (a moose in a bar) into a worse situation (a drunk moose in a bar). While the town couldn't outright ban owning a moose, they could ban letting a moose walk down a sidewalk, which, in turn, would prevent Pete's moose from moseying into the saloon. And that's exactly what they did.

STUNNED: Kids, stick with the Nerf guns. Real weapons are not as exciting as they look. They're loud, they're heavy, and they can result in serious injury or even death if you hold it the wrong way, which is too big of a risk for someone who can't even vote to take. Yes, stun guns count as weapons. At least, that's the case in the state of Alaska, where this buzzy device is considered a "defensive firearm." What's more? You can't sell them to children. Obvious? Perhaps. But if there's a law forbidding it, that means there was likely an incident that necessitated the law. Because remember, you can't always trust people to do the right thing, but if you make that thing illegal, you can at least increase the chances that they'll think about it.

SECRET SLINGSHOT: Federal law dictates that anyone over the age of eighteen can possess a firearm. Alaska law says, to hell with it. Give sixteen-year-olds guns. But you know what they can't have? Slingshots. Apparently, in one tiny Alaska town called Haines, carrying a concealed slingshot is actually illegal. Anyone desperate to do so has to acquire a permit, even if there's no ill intent in it. What, officer? I was just trying to hit two birds with one stone! Literally! That's no reason to arrest me!

TRAILER TRASH: It's fine to live in a trailer, as long as it's stationary. But the second that thing hits the road, you're in for some legal trouble. One obscure Alaska ordinance insists that "no person may occupy a house trailer while it is being moved upon a public street." Guess they don't want anyone accidentally tumbling out the front door when the driver suddenly screeches to a stop at an intersection.

BACK SEAT DRIVERS: Every dog wants to lounge in the back of a pickup, his ears flopping in the wind as his owner cruises down a snowy highway, but it's just not that simple. An untrained dog could leap out and attack someone, or leap headfirst into an oncoming car, or spot a moose and go running into the wilderness without warning. It's just too risky. Hoping to avoid headlines like "Who Let the Dogs Out: Canine Jumps Off Pickup, Goes Rogue," Alaska implemented a policy preventing anyone from transporting animals in the cargo bed. Section 9.36.150 states: "No person driving a motor vehicle shall transport any animal in the back of the vehicle in a space intended for any load on the vehicle on a street unless the space is enclosed or has side and tail walls to a height of at least forty-six inches extending vertically from the floor, or the animal is cross tethered to the vehicle, or is protected by a secured container or cage, in a manner which will prevent the animal from being thrown, falling or jumping from the vehicle." So, Bandit, it's either the back seat or shotgun. What's it going to be?

CALIFORNIA
Green Juice Nation

BE GENTLE: Every year in October, hundreds of monarch butterflies migrate to a little seaside town in California called Pacific Grove, where they nestle into the area's cypress and eucalyptus trees and hunker down for the winter. This area, nicknamed Butterfly Town USA, has become an official sanctuary for these colorful creatures, and people will travel hundreds of miles to get a glimpse of these little bug clusters. But if you choose to do so, you have to follow the rules, including one that says you cannot "molest" the butterflies.

Per the Pacific Grove legislature, "it is declared to be unlawful for any person to molest or interfere with, in any way, the peaceful occupancy of the monarch butterflies on their annual visit to the city of Pacific Grove, and during the entire time they remain within the corporate limits of the city, in whatever spot they may choose to stop in; provided, however, that if said butterflies should at any time swarm in, upon or near the private dwelling house or other buildings of a citizen of the city of Pacific Grove in such a way as to interfere with the occupancy and use of said dwelling and/or other buildings, that said butterflies may be removed, if possible, to another location upon the application of said citizen to the chief of police." Put another way, unless the butterflies swarm you like the killer birds in Alfred Hitchcock's titular horror film, leave them alone.

FANCY FROGS: In Angels Camp, California, there is an annual tradition known as the Calaveras Jumping Frog Jubilee in which residents of the city gather around to watch frogs jump across a stage and bet on who will jump the highest and the fastest. For locals, the competition—which takes place on the third weekend of May each year—is sacred; the days leading up to the big event are filled with scouring the forest for the perfect frog, then feeding and training said frog so that they may outleap their competitors. Even the state takes the competitions seriously. In the past few decades, they have implemented a number of laws meant to regulate such contests to make them safe for both the humans and the frogs.

One such law has attracted the attention of the internet, and that's article 2 of the fish and game code, which states that "any person may possess any number of live frogs to use in frog-jumping contests, but if such a frog dies or is killed, it must be destroyed as soon as possible, and may not be eaten or otherwise used for any purpose." That's right. If you participate in a frog-jumping contest, like the one in Angels Camp, and the frog dies, you are not allowed to eat it. You must find another way to dispose of the body. Flush it down the toilet. Drop-kick it into a lake. Light a raft on fire and push it out into the ocean. Whatever feels right.

SINK OR SWIM OR BIKE: Growing up in California means eating avocado like it's a separate food group, wearing a jacket when the temperature drops below sixty degrees, and skateboarding along surfaces that weren't meant for skateboarding. One such surface includes empty swimming pools, which, according to some sources, became a popular destination for skaters in the 1970s when the boarding culture was on the rise. Teenagers would sneak into empty swimming pools and use them as a makeshift half-pipe. In response, lawmakers decided to implement a rule preventing anyone from "biking in a swimming pool." Out of context, such a rule might sound silly, but when you remember how many swimming pools were infested with restless, hormonal teens, it all makes sense.

DON'T REACH FOR THE STARS: California's skies may be filled with smog, but they certainly won't be filled with kites. In the city of Walnut, it's illegal to "fly, above an altitude of ten feet above the ground, or near any electrical-conductive public utility wires or facilities, any kite or balloon which has a body or any parts, tail, string or ribbon made of any metallic or electrical conductive material." Keep those kites at nine feet or below, and you'll have smooth sailing.

HIDE AND REEK: Smell that? That's the smell of someone breaking the law. Chico, California, has an ordinance banning anyone from owning or storing "any green hide or any hide giving off an offensive odor." A hide is the heavy, raw skin of an animal often used to make coats or rugs that PETA will judge you for.

COME HERE, CANARY: Note to self: don't accidentally let your pet bird escape because if you do, you might end up wandering around the city, whistling for your precious canary at 6:00 a.m. and getting swiftly arrested. That's because, if you live in Berkeley, California, whistling for a lost canary before 7:00 a.m. is illegal. Not only because the law says so but also because doing so will get you some complaints from your neighbors for waking them up with earsplitting whistles at the crack of dawn.

COLORADO
High as a Mountain

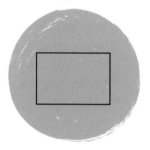

COUCH POTATO: There's a reason you don't put plush armchairs on the front lawn. They'll get destroyed by weather, infested with bugs, and heavily inspected by thrifters looking for their next project. They're simply not designed to be outdoors. Colorado is well aware of this fact. One of their biggest cities, Boulder, has even gone so far as to outlaw the practice. Under Section 5-4-16 of its municipal code, "no person shall place, use, keep, store, or maintain any upholstered furniture not manufactured for outdoor use, including, without limitation, upholstered chairs, upholstered couches, and mattresses, in any outside areas." Impacted most by this law is probably the area's college students, who can no longer enjoy the simple pleasure of waking up after a long night of partying on a beat-up couch in the backyard of a frat house.

BOULDERS IN BOULDER: Did you know you can't roll a boulder in Boulder? What sounds like a riddle is actually a city "public property" ordinance that bans any resident from rolling or throwing rocks haphazardly. Section 5-4-8 states that "no person shall roll, throw, or otherwise move any rocks or boulders on any public property. But this section does not apply to city employees acting within the scope of their employment." So, unless you're a geologist, a construction worker, or Sisyphus, you're not allowed to touch rocks in the city of Boulder. Don't even look at them. Don't even breathe on them.

DADDY DANDELIONS: He loves me, he loves me not. He plucks me, he plucks me not. He lets me grow taller than ten inches, he goes to jail. That's what's going through the head of every dandelion in the state of Colorado right now, because thanks to a 1957 law, it's illegal to let weeds of any kind—including "grass, brush or other rank or noxious vegetation" (which includes the little yellow flowers we talk to in elementary school)—to grow more than ten inches in height. Plants of this size can become a breeding ground for bugs, rodents, and other small mammals looking to settle down in a field of pretty flowers.

STOP, POLICE: No means no. We teach this lesson to our kids to ensure that they respect others. Coloradoans teach this lesson to their kids to help them avoid jail time. According to one ordinance in the Boulder, while it is totally legal to taunt a police officer, it becomes illegal the second said officer asks you to please, stop. Titled "Use of Fighting Words," the code says that "no person shall, with intent to harass, annoy, or alarm another, repeatedly insult, taunt, or challenge another in a manner likely to provoke a disorderly response. If the person to whom such insult, taunt, or challenge is directed is a police officer, there is no violation of this section until the police officer requests the person to cease and discontinue the conduct, but the person repeats or continues the conduct." We're not encouraging the harassment of the police, obviously, but know your rights: you can call their uniforms weird or mock their badges or poke fun at their batons, so long as they don't ever politely ask you to quit it.

BOMBS AWAY: The city of Aspen is known for its skiing resorts and rich tourists, but it's also known for something else: its strangely specific law against catapults. According to an ordinance passed in 1971, "it shall be unlawful for any person to throw any stone, snowball or other missile or discharge any bow, blowgun, slingshot, gun, catapult or other device upon or at any vehicle, building or other public or private property or upon or at any person or in any public way or place which is public in nature." While the mention of stones, snowballs, and guns certainly makes sense here, it's unclear why lawmakers felt the need to include catapults into the mix. Do Coloradoans have a penchant for these medieval devices? Is this a strange addiction they struggle with?

HAWAII
Your Dream Vacation

BILL BORED: Needing to advertise your upcoming feature film or questionable wellness product? Take out an ad in the paper. Print some posters. Launch a publicity stunt in the town square if you have to. Just please, for the love of God, don't make a billboard. One, because they're tacky, but two, because they're illegal in this sunny island state, and for the exact reason you think: they're an eyesore. They obstruct Hawaii's natural landscape and, therefore, are a threat to Hawaii's tourism industry. After all, people don't hop on a six-hour plane ride to see posters for *Transformers*. They do it to see the island's beautiful trees and oceanscapes and pretend for just a moment that they aren't at their desk jobs, huddled around a watercooler talking about the next finance presentation or the latest *Big Lebowski* remake. Don't ruin that for them.

BEACH BUM: It's OK to like drinking fine wine and taking long walks on the beach, as long as you do them separately. Because as much as advertisements like to make Hawaii seem like a Piña Colada paradise, there's one rule that prevents that fantasy from coming true: it's illegal to drink alcohol on the beach. In fact, it's illegal to have open containers in any public place, unless you want a three-hundred-dollar ticket and an encounter with the police. The good news, though? Booze cruises are totally a thing. So, if you need to drink on the water, spend that money on a boat trip instead and you can sip away all you want.

CAN YOU EAR THAT: Drug dealers have a variety of creative ways to let potential customers know they're carrying, like leaving pockets outturned or mean muggin' underneath a bridge. In Hawaii, though, they use a different system: dealers in the Aloha State nestle coins into their ears to let interested parties know that they've got the goods. Where this tactic came from is unclear—some believe it's tied to the state's long history with currency and how, in the 1900s, when the state was ordered to destroy their coinage, many residents decided to hide the trinkets in their ears to preserve them—but police have now caught on and have decided to ban the practice entirely in an effort to weed out the bad guys. At least, that's how the story goes—we couldn't find any evidence of the law on the books anywhere.

HAZARDOUS DRIVING: Most people turn their hazard lights on when they're preparing for a funeral procession or when they really need to run in and grab their morning iced coffee but there's just nowhere to park. But, if you pull away from that Dunkin' Donuts and forget that your hazards are blinking, you might be in for a rough afternoon because in Hawaii, it's against the law for a car in motion to have its hazards on. What do you do, then, when your car is malfunctioning, and you need to get off the road? Pull over as quickly as possible and pray that no one hits you, or find another way to get the attention of the drivers around you. A flare, maybe?

EYELID TATTOO: You cannot get a tattoo on your eyelid in Hawaii. While internet users love to throw this law around, there doesn't appear to be any solid evidence behind it, other than a few sources that claim it can only be done under the care of a licensed physician. While it's true that a licensed tattoo artist must be present, there doesn't appear to be any law regulating exactly what kind of tattoo you want to get on your body. So, if you want to plaster two black holes over your eyelids to give anyone who sees you nightmares, then go right ahead. No one's stopping you.

IDAHO
Po-Tay-Toes

HUNGRY, HUNGRY HUMANS: Cannibalism is illegal in Idaho. That's the good news. The bad news is that there are exceptions. Under chapter 50 of the state's legislature, fittingly titled "Mayhem," it's noted that eating another person's flesh is generally frowned upon, unless "the action was taken under extreme life-threatening conditions as the only apparent means of survival." In other words, you can eat someone else but only if you absolutely have to. What's worrying about this passage is that dangerously vague "life-threatening conditions." What does one consider life-threatening? Could some hangry defendant argue that it was necessary to eat their brother after only ten hours without food? In the moment, that kind of hunger might feel life-threatening, after all.

SCARY SNOWBALLS: "You'll shoot your eye out, kid!" While most recognize this as the phrase that haunts little Ralphie in the 1983 film *A Christmas Story*, others, like those from Rexburg, Idaho, may know it as the reason they can't throw snowballs at their friends in the wintertime. In this Western town, it's "unlawful for any person within the city limits ... to willfully or carelessly throw any stone, stick, snowball, egg, bomb, missile, or other substance whereby any person is hit, or any window broken, or any property injured or destroyed." In case you didn't catch that, this ordinance essentially says it's illegal to throw a snowball at another person, which begs the question: Isn't that the whole point? What else were snowballs made for? While the head of the Rexburg police department argues that the law was made to protect innocent people from ending up in the crosshairs of a snowball fight and getting hurt, some members of the town disagree with the ruling, which limits even snowball fights among friends, who just want to fling ice at each other until they can't feel their fingers anymore.

LOSE MY NUMBER: Maybe your boss just laid you off. Maybe your stock numbers just tanked. Maybe your mother-in-law just banned you from the annual Christmas white elephant party. Whatever it is, if you learned it while talking on a public telephone and you're tempted to smash the receiver against the wall over and over again in anger, think again. That's illegal in the great state of Idaho, where Statute 18-6801 says, "Every person who maliciously displaces, removes, injures or destroys any public telephone instrument or any part thereof or any equipment or facilities associated therewith, or who enters or breaks into any coin box associated therewith, or who willfully displaces, removes, injures or destroys any telegraph or telephone line, wire, cable, pole or conduit belonging to another or the material or property appurtenant thereto is guilty of a misdemeanor." There aren't many public telephones left in the world, but the ones that remain need to be respected, or else.

I'M YELLING TIMBER: The world is in a tricky position. While some people are desperate to slow the rate of deforestation and climate change, others, like your sixty-three-year-old boss who insists on printing out every email because computers "are just too hard," are unwittingly increasing the rate by choosing to kill every tree on the earth's surface rather than adapt to digital technologies. With such a powerful force (senior citizens) working against us, it's not surprising to hear that climate activists are conceiving of new ways to protect the planet. One such way that Idaho citizens have devised is spiking: a practice that involves slipping metal shards inside trees in an attempt to sabotage the logging process. These shards, when put through a wood-shredder, can not only get lodged inside the machines and break them, but they can also explode out of them like a bullet, injuring whoever is operating the device.

For this reason, the state has crafted new laws banning the practice, laws that come with heavy fines. One such law says that "any person who willfully, maliciously or mischievously drives or causes to be driven or imbedded any nail, spike or piece of iron, steel or other metallic substance, or any rock or stone, into any log or timber intended to be manufactured into boards, lath, shingles or other lumber, or to be marketed for such purpose, is punishable by imprisonment in the state prison not more than five (5) years or by imprisonment in the county jail not less than six (6) months, or by fine not to exceed $5000, in the discretion of the court." Tree huggers, take note: if you want to protect the planet, try a different tactic, unless you want to end up penniless and imprisoned for unintentionally killing some poor logger named Carl with a metal shard.

MISCHIEVOUS ANIMALS: If your fourteen-year-old golden retriever, Pancake, escapes his pen, you can probably assume that he's not a danger to society and that he'll turn up an hour later sitting under a sunbeam in the park. But if your two-month-old untrained Doberman with a history of chomping off limbs escapes, then you should probably call the authorities before someone ends up dead, or worse. If you don't, then the state of Idaho has no choice but to punish you, per the rules outlined in Section 18-5808 of its legislature. Passed in 1937, it states that "if the owner of a mischievous animal, knowing its propensities, willfully suffers it to go at large, or keeps it without ordinary care, and such animal, while so at large, or while not kept with ordinary care, kills any human being who has taken all the precautions which circumstances permitted, or which a reasonable person would ordinarily take in the same situation, is guilty of a felony."

WHITE CANE: Unless they've been cast as Helen Keller in a local theater production, no person should ever impersonate a blind individual. Why? A number of reasons, but mainly, vision-impaired people have enough problems—they don't need to add "contesting with fake blind people" to the list. That's why one statute in Idaho prohibits the use of white canes—a device frequently used by the vision-impaired to signal their disability to outsiders. The rule says that "no person, except those wholly or partially blind, shall carry or use on any street, highway, or in any other public place a cane or walking stick which is white in color, or white tipped with red." See the problem?

MONTANA
It's All Natural

ALL THE WORLD'S NOT A STAGE: The most exciting part of any concert is the moment when the performer leaps off stage and runs around the arena, high-fiving strangers and snapping selfies with screaming teens. It makes you wonder: What do performances look like in Montana? Because in the capital of this frigid state, entertainers are legally barred from leaving the stage for the duration of their performance. Section 3-301 of the Billings code of ordinances insists that "the owner or proprietor of an establishment selling alcoholic beverages for on-premises consumption may permit in the establishment instrumental and/or vocal music or entertainment and/or radio and television entertainment . . . provided, that all live entertainment as herein specified shall be performed on a platform or other exclusive area provided for such purpose, and no entertainer or performer whether male or female shall be permitted to leave such platform or area while entertaining or performing."

It's hard to say what's most interesting about this law: Is it the fact that it prohibits offstage performances? Or that it specifically says neither males nor females can break the law, as if to say, "No, tipsy guys are not the only ones drunkenly stumbling into crowds mid-song."

GET RID OF RATS: Rats. They're smaller than dogs, cuter than snakes, and a dash more exciting than fish. Despite all of that, though, they're not the most popular pet in the world. They're not even the most popular pet in the United States. (That distinction goes to dogs, to nobody's surprise.) And they're definitely not the most popular pet in Montana, where owning a rat (or even giving one away as a present) is illegal. As noted by Section 4-304 of the state's legislature, "It is unlawful for any person to sell, offer for sale, harbor, raise or give away rats as pets, toys, premiums, novelties, or for any other purpose except as feed for reptiles or birds of prey or both, or as hereinafter set forth; or to bring or transport the same into the city." If you're determined to get something that's small, hairy, and loves cheese, consider mice or your little brother instead.

PLENTY OF FISH IN THE SEA: Don't believe everything on the internet, including this old wives' tale which says that unmarried women are not allowed to fish alone in Montana. While fishing alone (or really, doing anything alone) as a woman in the middle of nowhere is probably not safe, there's no actual law against it, despite the many online sources that swear by the law's existence. Supposedly, the Montana state website once mentioned that "in Montana, it is illegal for married women to go fishing alone on Sundays, and illegal for unmarried women to fish alone at all," but any evidence of such a claim has since been removed.

SPEED DIAL: To avoid the embarrassment brought on by accidentally butt-dialing 911 or your mother-in-law, the city of Billings, Montana, created a law banning speed dial, or any device that "automatically dial[s] any number, emergency or otherwise." It's also illegal "to program or cause any pre-recorded taped message to be played to any number," which means giving out a fake number to creepy guys in bars that connects to a prerecorded message telling them to bugger off is, unfortunately, against the law. Find another way to scare them off. Talking about marriage usually does the trick.

FOLF: Frisbee? Fine. Golf? OK. Frisbee and golf? No way, Jose. In Helena, Montana, "folfing"—a sport that combines frisbee and golf by asking players to toss discs onto pegs—is prohibited, according to local ordinance 5-13-2, which states "no person shall play or engage in the game of folf or throw a golf disc at nighttime in any area within the business improvement district that has not been sanctioned as a designated folf course by the city." Yes, that means the word *folf* is recorded in an actual legal document. Take that in. It doesn't get much better than that.

NEVADA
What Happens in Vegas . . .

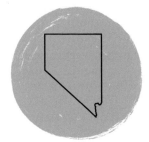

SHOP 'TIL YOU DROP: You'll see a lot of things on the sidewalks of Reno: wealthy tourists in winter sports gear, wealthy tourists in summer sports gear, wealthy tourists in general. But one thing you won't see is a person lying down because, according to the city's administrative code, "sitting or lying on the public sidewalks in the Downtown Reno Regional Center interferes with the primary purposes of the public sidewalks, threatens public safety and damages the public welfare" and is therefore off-limits. So, if you're tired, find a hotel room. If you want to tan, go to a park. If your feet are bloodied from walking around in too-tight boots and you simply need a break, cut off your feet. You have options.

UP AND AT 'EM: When you're the home of one of the best skiing and snowboarding resorts in the world, you must pay close attention to your winter sports laws or else risk having someone do something stupid, like throw a snowball filled with razors or challenge a police officer to a duel with a ski pole. That's why there's a whole section of the Nevada state legislature dedicated to "safety of participants in outdoor sports," one which includes a rule prohibiting people from throwing items off or at a ski lift. Because when people are zipping down a mountain, the last thing they're doing is looking up to avoid incoming shoes or sandwiches or other flying objects.

HULA-HOOP HULLABALOO: For many, Vegas seems like a virtually lawless place where you can party until 4:00 a.m., drive a cop car into a lake, and fall asleep with an alligator in a bathtub with absolutely no consequences. But that's not entirely true. In some areas of Vegas—specifically, inside the countless pedestrian malls across the city—there are rules. Strict rules. Weird rules. Including one that bans Hula-Hoop contests, or really any special event or contest involving unicycles, skateboards, in-line skates, and other items that might end with someone losing an eye.

VROOM VROOM: While getting drunk and riding around in a clown car might sound like a good idea at the time (it always does), avoid it the next time you're in Vegas unless you want to get in trouble with the Las Vegas police. One city ordinance bans the use of toy vehicles on roadways, sidewalks, intersections . . . basically anywhere that might be filled with people, which, in Vegas, is pretty much everywhere.

HUMP DAY: Back in the nineteenth century, when explorers started pushing into the Western part of the United States, they encountered an unfortunate problem: a whole lotta desert. Without roads to drive on, these settlers had to find another way of getting around these sandy terrains. So, they turned to camels, whose reputation for carrying large loads and enduring long journeys made them valuable.

Over time, the use of camels started to spread but so, too, did rumors of their negative behaviors. Camels, it turns out, do not play nice with others. They spit, they charge at things, and they emit strong odors that drive most other animals away. For this reason, lawmakers in 1875 crafted an ordinance banning camels and dromedaries (one-humped camels) from walking along highways: "From and after the passage of this Act it shall be unlawful for the owner or owners of any camel or camels, dromedary or dromedaries, to permit them to run at large on or about the public roads or highways of this State. If any owner or owners of any camel or camels, dromedary or dromedaries, shall, knowingly or willfully permit any violation of this Act, he or they shall be deemed guilty of a misdemeanor and shall be arrested." When the camel caravans disappeared in the early 1900s, so too did this law.

OREGON

It's a Vibe

OPEN-DOOR POLICY: You know that scene in movies when a person is bicycling down the street, minding their own business, and then all of a sudden, the door of a parked car swings open, jutting into the biker's path and sending them flying in a way that's both comical but also definitely life-threatening? That probably first happened in Oregon. The state implemented a law in 1983 forbidding anyone from leaving their car door open for too long.

GEE-WHIZZ: You're five hours into a week-long road trip, alone, in the middle of nowhere, with not a bathroom in sight. A tingle creeps into your bladder, making your legs dance uncomfortably beneath the steering wheel. For a moment, you consider pulling over and discharging in a bush, but the land is arid and there's nowhere to hide. That's when you see it: an empty water bottle rolling around on the floor of your passenger seat. As the pressure in your bladder starts to build, you make a decision and pee into the bottle. Sweet release. Then, when you think no one is watching, you eek the window open and tilt the bottle into the wind, dumping the liquid onto the concrete.

You may think this simple, desperate act is nothing more than a quick fix, but in Oregon, it's something much, much worse: a crime. As the law states: "A person commits the offense of improperly disposing of human waste if the person is operating or riding in a motor vehicle and the person throws, puts or otherwise leaves a container of urine or other human waste on or beside the highway."

CALL YOUR DAD, YOU'RE IN A CULT: Professor Snape would have no problem teaching the Dark Arts in this Western state, so long as he stayed away from anything resembling occult magic—that is, any practice rooted in mysticism or other unscientific beliefs. In Yamhill, Oregon, there is a whole section in their municipal code dedicated to the occult. It reads that "the use or practice of fortune telling, astrology, phrenology, palmistry, clairvoyance, mesmerism, spiritualism, or any other practice or practices generally recognized to be unsound and unscientific" is illegal, especially if it aims "to reveal or analyze past incidents or events, to analyze or define the character or personality of a person, to foretell or reveal the future, to locate by such means lost or stolen property, [or] to give advice or information concerning any matter or event." Stick with economics, or another useful degree.

ICE ICE BABY: The children are our future. That's why it's important that we protect them at all costs. No, not by stopping climate change or setting them up for future success—by preventing them from walking into open iceboxes. In Vale, Oregon, Section 4.4.5 of the city code outlaws "abandoned iceboxes" with the following rule: "No person shall leave in a place accessible to children an abandoned or discarded icebox, refrigerator or similar container without first removing the door." The section goes on to regulate other potentially dangerous setups like unguarded machinery, quarries, cisterns, or lumber yards. What are the babies of Oregon up to these days . . .

THEY'RE ALREADY DEAD: Section 166.645 of the Oregon legislature gets right to the point: "Hunting in cemeteries is prohibited." No elaboration. No footnotes. Just "no hunting in a place where everything is already dead."

UTAH
Mormonville

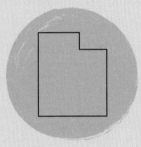

ALL BARK, NO BITE: Sorry, Mike Tyson. You're going to have to change your ways if you're planning on boxing in Utah. This pious Western state has very particular rules about fighting matches, including one that bans the use of biting. You'd think this would be obvious, but not in Utah, where there is a whole section on the rules of boxing, just in case anyone decides to go rogue and nibble on some ears, "intentionally inflict serious bodily injury upon an opponent through . . . the expulsion of a projectile" or utilize "direct, intentional, and forceful strikes to the eyes, groin area, [or] Adam's apple area of the neck."

UNHAPPY HOUR: Here's a secret: if you want people to buy less of something, just up the price and slash all discounts until the pain inflicted on their wallets outweighs the desire swelling in their hearts. It's one of the basic rules of capitalism, one that Utah has cleverly hijacked for their own purposes. In their effort to sober up the state (this is the land of Mormons, after all—the caffeine-averse, marriage-loving, substance-hating religious group that dominates the area), the lawmakers of Utah have banned the discounting of booze. That means no happy hours, no brunch mimosa specials, and no "I just turned twenty-one, can I have a free drink" deals. Why? Because discounting alcohol encourages drinking, of course. The Utah Department of Public Safety quite literally says this on their FAQ page, noting, "As far as liquor licensees and liquor sales are concerned, . . . happy hours or any other promotion which discounts beer or liquor prices is prohibited, as is anything else which promotes over consumption."

CATASTROPHIC: What your best friend considers a catastrophe and what the world considers a catastrophe can greatly differ. For example, your friend may think that her boyfriend refusing to put on the ugly Christmas sweater that she made him for their holiday card photoshoot is a catastrophe while the rest of the world may just call that "totally reasonable." Regardless of how one defines the word, there's one thing that doesn't change, and that's Utah's policy on "catastrophes," which states that "causing a catastrophe is a first-degree felony if the person causes the catastrophe knowingly." Of course, the law goes on to identify a catastrophe as an "explosion, fire, flood, avalanche, collapse of a building, or other harmful or destructive force or substance" or a significant event caused by a weapon of mass destruction, so the rule is not as vague as it might initially appear. But it's far more fun to imagine someone getting arrested for overreacting to their significant other's mysterious text rather than, you know, causing a deadly event, so we're going to stick with that.

EMERGENCY DRINK: No, your mother-in-law forgetting to bring the rice pudding on Christmas is not "an emergency." You cannot run to the store, buy a bottle of Rosé, and chug it inside the closest restroom you can find while texting your family "something came up, go on without me." That's not a reasonable response and also, for the record, it's illegal. In the state of Utah, you're not allowed to purchase alcohol during an emergency, whatever it may be. Now, what constitutes as an emergency is up to the discretion of the governor, so if you're desperate to drink away your rice pudding rage, take it up with them before you black out and ruin Christmas again.

GOING ONCE, GOING TWICE: When car dealerships want to attract customers, they put a wacky waving inflatable tube man out front. When an auction wants to attract customers, they use . . . tambourines? This, at least, seems to be what the state of Utah is afraid of, because in 1999, Salt Lake County implemented a rule that regulates how auctions can market their events. It says that "all auctioneers are forbidden to . . . make or cause to be made noisy acclamations such as ringing of bells, blowing of whistles, or otherwise, though not enumerated here, through the streets in advertising their sales; and no bellman or crier, drum or fife or other musical instrument or noisemaking means of attracting the attention of passersby, except the customary auctioneer's flags, shall be employed or suffered to be used at or near any place of sale or at or near any auction room, or near any auction whatsoever." In short, if you want to advertise your auction, leave the flutes and fifes at home. The inflatable tube man will work just fine.

WASHINGTON
The Rainy Day Special

X-RAY VISION: Picture this: you're at a shoe store, trying to find the perfect pair of Reeboks to go with your new outfit, and you slip on a pair that appears to be your size but after walking up and down the aisle a few times, you realize that you're not quite sure. So, what do you do? Use an X-ray to scan your foot, obviously. That must've happened at some point in Washington's history, because there's a law prohibiting "the operation or maintenance of any x-ray, fluoroscopic, or other equipment or apparatus employing roentgen rays, in the fitting of shoes or other footwear." Why was this law made? It's unclear, but there's a story in there somewhere.

DO I HAVE YOUR ATTENTION?: Why is window-shopping so addictive? Because most chain stores hire experts to literally design their display cases to attract eyeballs, whether it's through strangely dressed mannequins or over-the-top festive decor. The only items off-limits, at least in the state of Washington, are those that are hypnotic. Literally. In the city of Everett, Washington, "it is unlawful for any hypnotist or mesmerist, or other person, to exhibit or display, or permit to be exhibited or displayed, any subject of any hypnotist or mesmerist, or any person while under the influence of or alleged influence of hypnotism or mesmerism, in any window or public place outside of the hall or theater where such hypnotist or mesmerist is giving his entertainment or exhibition." In other words, it is illegal to hypnotize anyone outside of a theater, whether that's a public park, a crowded street, or a storefront.

SASQUATCH: Unless you've been living under a rock, you've probably heard stories about the legendary Sasquatch a.k.a. Bigfoot: an ape-like cryptid believed to roam the Pacific Northwest. Though the first official mention of the name Bigfoot occurred around 1958 when the *Humboldt Times* featured a story about loggers in California who had spotted mysteriously large footprints on the ground in a nearby forest, the creature is believed to be much older. For this reason, Skamania County has actually prohibited the murder of Bigfoot. Well, that and the fact that, when this ordinance was put into place in 1969, it was April Fools' and lawmakers wanted a funny headline for that day's newspaper. The joke's on them, though, because as more "evidence" of Bigfoot began to surface, the number of hunters flocking to the town to hunt down the creature increased, forcing officials to actually start enforcing the rule.

STAY INSIDE: Those with persnickety bosses may balk at the notion of staying home when sick, but if you live in Washington state, you might not have a choice. Section RCW 70.54.050 of the Washington state legislature prohibits going outside when ill: "Every person who shall willfully expose himself to another, or any animal affected with any contagious or infectious disease, in any public place or thoroughfare, except upon his or its necessary removal in a manner not dangerous to the public health; and every person so affected who shall expose any other person thereto without his knowledge, shall be guilty of a misdemeanor." If, for example, you learned that you had an infectious disease like COVID-19 and you decided to go to your grandma's birthday party anyway, you could be fined for exposing others to your ailment and putting your sweet old Nana in danger.

OPEN DOORS: Anyone who says they have never pushed a door that said "Pull" is lying. This common mistake has led to countless broken noses and bruised egos, leading some places, like Washington, to implement ordinances limiting the use of confusing doors. One law in Washington literally prohibits the installation of outward-swinging doors on public buildings.

WYOMING
Did You See That Moose?

DARK WATERS: Similar to Indiana's "hands alone" law, there's a Wyoming statute that prohibits anyone from fishing with a gun. Rather, it's illegal to "take, wound or destroy any fish of Wyoming with a fire-arm." It's unclear whether or not "wounding" encompasses emotional wounds.

SLIZZARD SKIING: As far as sports go, skiing is relatively safe. The average rate of injury is 2 people per 1,000 skiers. (Hockey, for comparison, has around 4 injuries per 1,000, and football has 8 injuries per 1,000.) However, those numbers go down the toilet when you add illegal substances into the mix. After all, it's very easy to slam into a tree when you're busy drunkenly giggling at the ski lift. Thankfully for everyone, Wyoming had the forethought to recognize this potential hazard and created a law to prevent it. Statute 6-9-301 says that "no person shall move uphill on any passenger tramway or use any ski slope or trail while such person's ability to do so is impaired by the consumption of alcohol or by the use of any illicit controlled substance or other drug." Doing so can result in a misdemeanor, a fine, and probably a few broken limbs.

HOLD THE DOOR: Sure, fences are mostly used to keep things out, but they can also be used to keep things in. Just ask your neighbor, who cowers every time they pass the barking dog in your yard. But not to fear. Wyoming has it covered. Buried within the state's 2013 statutes is a law banning anyone from neglecting to close their fence door: "a person is guilty of a misdemeanor punishable by a fine of not more than seven hundred fifty dollars ($750.00) if he opens and neglects to close a gate or replace bars in a fence which crosses a private road or a river, stream or ditch."

WINE AND MINE: When you're two miles beneath the surface of the earth, breathing in soot in the dark for hours on end, it's only natural that you'd want to find some way to liven up the experience. Maybe you decide to start a game of sardines. Or maybe you challenge a peer to an ice-pick duel. Or perhaps you smuggle in a flask of whiskey and drunkenly stab at rocks for two hours. Two of these outlets are perfectly acceptable. One of them is not. In fact, one of them could land you in jail for up to a year.

According to public safety statute 35-10-402, "whoever shall, while under the influence of intoxicating liquor, enter any mine, smelter, metallurgical works, machine shops or sawmills, or any of the buildings connected with the operation of the same in Wyoming where miners or workmen are employed or whoever shall carry or haul any intoxicating liquor into the same or any logging or grading camp shall be deemed guilty of a misdemeanor and upon conviction shall be fined in any sum not exceeding five hundred dollars ($500.00) to which may be added imprisonment in the county jail for a term not exceeding one (1) year."

SPITTIN' SESSION: Teachers do a lot for this world. They dedicate their free time to schoolwork, put up with hormonal teenagers and their dramatic outbursts, and endure endless parent-teacher conferences, all for shockingly little pay. Not many people respect the work they do, but Cheyenne is different. The capital of Wyoming actually has a rule on the books that outlaws spitting on the steps of public buildings. It states: "No person shall spit upon the floor, walls or steps of any school, theater, hall, assembly room, public building or conveyance."

IT'S ART: Did you know every state has an agency dedicated to promoting and installing new art? The National Assembly of State Arts Agencies is the organization responsible for such groups, and every year they find new ways to encourage the states to incorporate artwork into their communities. While some states are more open to such encouragement, others need a little more convincing, usually in the form of pesky laws. One such law from Wyoming insists that buildings that cost over 100,000 dollars must display art and allocate 1 percent of their funds to doing so. As added incentive, state funds can be made available for this, assuming the art piece itself doesn't cost over 100,000 dollars. If it does, then everything else is out of pocket and you're on your own. Pay for your own decorations.

THE TERRITORIES
Close, but no Cigar

You know how camps hire middle schoolers over the summer to serve as "counselors-in-training" so they can learn the ropes and eventually become regular counselors? That's sort of what territories are. The island territories, which the United States has collected over the years like playing cards, have their own governments and systems, and are constantly working to fulfill the conditions required to request state-hood, namely: having 60,000 or more citizens, drafting an "acceptable" state constitution, agreeing to teach English in schools, etc. Once these benchmarks have been met, territories can shoot their shot with Congress, who can confirm or deny them at their leisure.

The United States has two commonwealths (Puerto Rico and Northern Marianas Islands) and three territories (Guam, American Samoa, and US Virgin Islands). While small, these little islands are overflowing with personality and history. Here's to hoping that one day their determination will pay off, and they'll no longer be just "the place your boss goes to vacation on a budget."

AMERICAN SAMOA

Closer to Australia
Than You Think

I VOTE TO CHANGE THIS DUMB LAW: With around 55,000 people to its name, American Samoa is filled with gorgeous hiking spots and shopping centers (no sales tax!), it's a hidden jewel for anyone looking for a cheap place to live out the rest of their days. Sounds perfect, right? Well, there's one catch: those born in American Samoa can live on the mainland United States, serve in the military, and hold United States passports . . . but they're not considered American citizens. Instead, they get a fancy alternative title—US Nationals—that earns them almost all of the same rights except, you know, the right to work in the United States and the right to vote. To be honest, though, none of the territories can vote—at least not in presidential elections—so maybe American Samoa isn't so special after all.

GUAM
Middle of Nowhere

V-CARD: For many US citizens, chastity is still an important value (and a booming business—homemade chastity belts on Etsy go for upwards of 130 dollars). Guamanians—residents of the far-flung US island—have even incorporated their devotion into their legal system. In this territory, if you lie about your virginity to your spouse, not only can your spouse demand an annulment, but also they can have the marriage deemed invalid from its inception. Section 3106 of its legislature goes a little something like this: "Neither party to a contract to marry is bound by a promise made in ignorance of the other's want of personal chastity, and either is released there from by unchaste conduct on the part of the other unless both parties participate therein." Thankfully, this law was updated in the late 2010s so that it now only applies on a case-by-case basis.

NORTHERN MARIANA ISLANDS
Pretty for Its Own Good.

Northern Mariana Islands earns the distinction of being just too gosh darn normal. We couldn't find any blasphemous laws worth including.

PUERTO RICO
Don't Mess with El Cuco

DRINKING CLASS: Most teenagers in the United States in pursuit of booze do one of two things: steal alcohol from their parents' cabinet or flee to Canada where the drinking age is eighteen (or nineteen, depending on the province). But there is a third option, one that is much more appealing for anyone who doesn't want to lose their toes to frostbite just to have a sip of Bud Lite: Puerto Rico. This US territory has a drinking age of just eighteen, not to mention miles and miles of crystal-clear oceans and a tropical vibe that will make you think you're somewhere exotic. So, skip the frigid temperatures of Canada and jet to this little island next time you're hankering for a legal Piña Colada— which was actually invented in this commonwealth.

MAGIC SCHOOL BUS: Don't get into a car with a stranger, kids, unless the car says "school bus" on the side. Then it's probably fine. That's the logic Puerto Ricans follow, anyway. On this island, authorized school buses must display a sign reading "School Bus" with letters at least eight inches tall. Supposedly, this is to prevent awkward misunderstandings between thirteen-year-olds looking for their ride to school and twenty-five-year-olds looking for their friend's birthday party bus.

HEY THERE, STUD: Studded tires are wheels that have metal pieces embedded in the tread to help add traction during colder months, when snow, ice, and frozen gravel gathers on the ground and conspires to crash your car. These devices are helpful winter accessories, which makes it all the more strange that they're banned in Puerto Rico, which hasn't seen snowfall since, well, ever.

US VIRGIN ISLANDS
Welcome to the Caribbean

MONGOOSE MONEY: You may know *mongoose* as the funny word makes your toddler giggle, but there's so much more to this creature that. These slim, weasel-y creatures can be found in Africa, Southern Asia, and the US Virgin Islands, where they rule with an iron thumb. Don't underestimate their stubby legs: these ferrets-on-steroids are famous for their ability to hunt, sometimes even decimating entire species. This behavior is especially bad on the US Virgin Islands, where their killing sprees have driven the snake population into the ground (to the delight of some). To combat this, the area put a bounty on these squirrely animals, offering twenty-five cents per dead mongoose. But, understanding that such a scheme could be abused, they added a clause to the law: "Whoever breeds the mongoose for the purpose of: obtaining the bounty prescribed by this section shall be fined not more than $25, and all the mongooses in his possession shall be confiscated and destroyed."

DRINK 'N' DRIVE: Most states in the United States have some version of an open-container law. While some are less strict than others (in Mississippi, you can literally drink an alcoholic beverage while driving), the US Virgin Islands take the award for loosest . . . because their open-container laws don't exist. In this island nation, you can drink in your car, on the beach, in your car on the beach, you name it. So, enjoy it! But don't enjoy it too much. It's still illegal to drive drunk. Obviously.

WASHINGTON, DC
Where Everyone Works in Politics

DANCING QUEEN: There are rumors floating around the internet about a strange Washington, DC, ruling that prevents people from dancing for more than twelve hours straight. That is, unfortunately, just a rumor—there appears to be no evidence of such a law. However, there is evidence of another anti-dancing statute: according to the Legal Information Institute, there is one National Capital Region ruling that forbids anyone from "demonstrating" in areas including the Jefferson Memorial.

The meaning of "demonstrating" and whether dancing falls under that umbrella came to a head in 2008 when a woman named Mary Brooke Oberwetter and seventeen of her friends decided to honor

Thomas Jefferson's birthday by engaging in a silent, expressive dance near his DC memorial. Officer Kenneth Hilliard of the United States Park Police noticed the activity and asked Oberwetter to stop; she refused and was promptly arrested. The subsequent court case ruled that, because dancing tends to attract attention, it falls under the category of demonstration which, as defined by the law, is "likely to draw a crowd or onlookers." Oberwetter tried to repeal the case later on to no avail. In his ruling, the judge Thomas Griffith offered a small dose of sass, noting in his footnotes that, by the way, Thomas Jefferson discouraged the celebration of his birthday and only ever celebrated America's birthday: the Fourth of July. So, take that, Mary.

WEATHERING THE WEATHER: On September 4, 2019, President Donald Trump did something that was objectively a little stupid. While talking to reporters about the path of Hurricane Dorian, he presented a map featuring an outline of the hurricane's path, including a Sharpie-drawn extension lumping Alabama into the mix. One problem: Alabama was never going to be hit. The president had falsely tweeted out earlier in the week that the state was in Dorian's line of fire when in reality, the state was not in danger. To avoid looking silly, Trump tried to save face by circling Alabama on the map. But in doing so, he did something far worse: he broke the law.

Yes, it's true. According to 18 US Code § 2074 (which is technically a federal law, but hey, federal laws are born in DC, so it counts), anyone who "knowingly issues or publishes any counterfeit weather forecast or warning of weather conditions falsely representing such forecast or warning . . . shall be fined under this title or imprisoned not more than ninety days, or both." So, when Donald etched that additional black

bubble inside the walls of the Oval Office, he was technically breaking the law, as many litigious weathermen were quick to point out on social media the following day.

KICK ROCKS: Tomatoes are multipurpose. When mashed, they make a great pizza topping. When juiced, they complete a Bloody Mary. And when thrown, they splatter. DC residents are likely aware of this last one, considering the use of hard projectiles like rocks are forbidden within its borders. The rule goes that it is unlawful "for any person or persons within the District of Columbia to throw any stone or other missile in any street, avenue, alley, road, or highway, or open space, or public square, or enclosure, or to throw any stone or other missile from any place into any street, avenue, road, or highway, alley, open space, public square, or enclosure, under a penalty of not more than $500 for every such offense." In other words, no throwing rocks in DC, no matter how many disgruntled politicians are blocking your commute. Stick with fruit.

PICTURES LAST LONGER: Hoping to take a cute tourist picture with your family in front of the White House? You better plan ahead. Chapter 24 of the DC municipal regulations states that no photographer shall remain in one place longer than five minutes. Now, of course, this rule was not intended to be widely applied: no police officer is going to arrest you for taking the extra time to perfect your family photo or scouting out that hot senator you've been waiting all year to see. This law was designed to stop street photographers who try to trick tourists into spending their entire vacation budget on a picture with a George Washington doppelganger.

DUEL YOU COWARD: On February 24, 1838, Kentucky representative William Graves presented Maine representative Jonathan Cilley with a letter from one of Cilley's constituents. Cilley refused to accept the letter, prompting Graves to challenge Cilley to a duel. The men fought for three rounds before Graves ultimately killed his opponent. The incident inspired Congress to draft a bill prohibiting "the giving or accepting within the District of Columbia, of a challenge to fight a duel, and for the punishment thereof." Duels, of course, continued to happen in Washington, but at least Congress can say they tried.

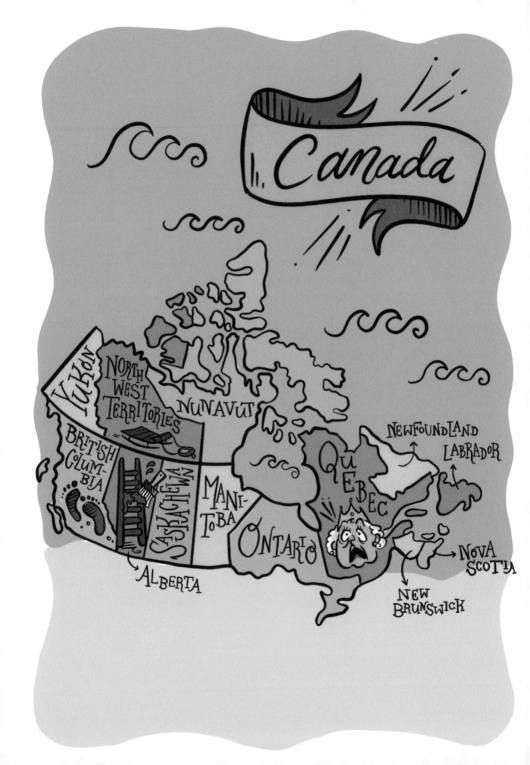

CANADA
It's Aboot Time

Canada. It's the place where all Americans joke about moving to when the political climate gets bad, where teenagers visit on the weekend to indulge in a quick legal drink, and where film productions scurry off to when they need to cut costs and don't mind freezing their butts off to do it. Composed of three territories and ten provinces, this notoriously cold northern country may look nice (its people certainly are) but behind those friendly smiles and that maple syrup enthusiasm are strange habits, some of which have resulted in laws even weirder than those in the states.

FEDERAL LAW
Betcha Didn't Know Canada Had Monarchs

SCREAM QUEEN: You might want to leave the queen out of your Halloween plans, unless you want up to fourteen years in jail. That's because in Canada—a constitutional monarchy ruled by Queen Elizabeth II—it is illegal to scare the queen. Or, rather, Her Majesty. Section 49 of the country's federal criminal code claims that anyone "who wilfully, in the presence of Her Majesty, (a) does an act with intent to alarm Her Majesty or to break the public peace, or (b) does an act that is intended or is likely to cause bodily harm to Her Majesty, is guilty of an indictable offence and liable to imprisonment for a term not exceeding fourteen years." The law dates back to 1842, when (rumor has it) a British man trying to conjure a good laugh pointed a gun at Queen Victoria, who was so displeased by the whole event that she requested a nationwide rule against it. Talk about a bad sport. The law was repealed in 2018.

ALBERTA
Insta-worthy

BROAD STROKES: Brown is such a boring color. Wouldn't you agree? Seriously, think of something brown. Does it elicit any sort of excitement in you? Brown bear, brown poop, brown egg. Now imagine if those items were a nice shade of periwinkle. Or cerulean. Or emerald. Doesn't that sound nice? Consider a wooden ladder. A dull, beige wooden ladder. Wouldn't you want to spruce it up a bit by adding a coat of crimson paint? Yes. Well, assuming you don't live in Alberta, Canada, you're perfectly within your right to do so. However, if you are a resident of this southern province, you are a bit limited in your ability to redesign your decor. This area has a very specific prohibition against painting ladders. Section 126 of its municipal code literally says, "a person must not paint a wooden ladder." No reason is given.

SKATER BOY: You know you have a good dad when, in the wintertime, he goes out to the backyard, pushes aside all the snow, and single-handedly creates an ice rink for you to twirl around in. Alberta dads are free to continue this tradition, as long as the rink doesn't extend out into the street because, thanks to one bylaw in the city of Wetaskiwin, it is illegal to "skate upon a roadway."

BRITISH COLUMBIA
Bear Aware

MAKE IT GO BOOM: In 1986, the Space Shuttle Challenger had just disintegrated over the skies of California, Halley's Comet was blasting through the atmosphere, and the Cold War was nearing an end. Of course, no one knew that at the time, and many feared the tensions between America and Russia were still palpable and many still feared the possibility of a nuclear war, including the town of Smithers in British Columbia, who hated the prospect so much, they went ahead and banned nuclear weapons from their area entirely. Bylaw 771 declared (on the International Day of Peace, no less) that the town of Smithers would become a Nuclear Weapons Free Zone. It noted that "by declaring itself to be a Nuclear Weapons Free Zone, the Town of Smithers symbolically conveys to the leaders of the world the act of opposition of the citizens of Smithers to the continuation of the nuclear arms race." Who knew we could stop nuclear war by just saying no?

BALLOONS OR BUST: Victoria, Canada, doesn't care if you have other talents. When you sign up to do a job, you do that job and you get out, end of story. This rule applies mostly to balloon artists who, in this area of British Columbia, are forbidden from doing anything other than balloon art. The law bluntly states that "if a street entertainer is a balloon artist, then the street entertainer shall not perform . . . unless the performance consists of the construction of balloons."

MANITOBA
Winterpeg

WELL, WELL, WHEEL: Snow Lake in Manitoba is a funny place. Not only does it boast a population of nine hundred people, but also it promises to impound the bicycles, tricycles, and unicycles of any citizen who doesn't pay the annual licensing fee for these vehicles. How much is this annual licensing fee? A whopping two dollars. Seems like a harsh punishment for such a trivial amount of money, but hey, we don't make the rules.

NOT MY SIDEWALK: Like most cities, Winnipeg in Manitoba has a team of people responsible for clearing the streets after a snowstorm or flurry. But unlike most cities, Winnipeg is picky about which streets get to be cleaned. According to its sidewalk cleaning bylaw, "All persons owning or occupying property abutting the street or streets listed in Schedule 'A' hereto, shall remove or cause to be removed and cleared away snow, ice, dirt, or other obstructions from any sidewalk adjoining their property such removal to be completed within forty-eight (48) hours of the time when the snow, ice, dirt or other obstruction was formed or deposited thereon." Listed in Schedule A are two chunks of the city: The west side of Osborne Street between River Avenue and Stradbrook Avenue and the east side of Osborne Street between River Avenue and Stradbrook Avenue. The north and the south have to fend for themselves.

NEW BRUNSWICK

Try Not to Hit a Deer

SNAKE SCARF: In 2013, two young boys were sleeping in the living room of their friend's home when an escaped African python slipped into their beds, coiled around their bodies, and strangled them to death. Jean-Claude Savoie—the father of the boys' friend and the owner of the home—also ran the reptile store on the first floor. He was charged with negligence after it was discovered that the snake had escaped its enclosure and slithered up the ventilation system and into Savoie's living room.

This traumatizing story is relevant because it sparked a wave of new laws in the area related to reptile ownership and how creatures like snakes and lizards can be displayed in public. For example, in Fredericton, New Brunswick, it is now illegal to "wear" a snake in public. Or, more specifically: "no person shall have, keep or possess a snake or other reptile upon the street or in any public place." That means no street performers, snake charmers, or randos walking around with boa constrictors draped across their shoulders.

SPLISH-SPLASH: There's a moment in every rom-com where a down-in-the-dumps character decides to take a walk in the rain to wallow in their sorrow, only to be splashed in the face by a wave of water created by a passing car. Perhaps this is why there aren't any movies set in Moncton, Canada. In this southern city, there is a law stating that it is illegal to "drive a motor vehicle on any street so as to splash water, mud or snow on a pedestrian." Not even if it's someone you hate. Not even if you want a good laugh.

NEWFOUNDLAND AND LABRADOR
Skeet City

LIKE CATNIP: Cats are unpredictable creatures. Buy them a warm, fuzzy bed, and they'll curl up in a discarded cardboard box. Feed them delicious food, and they'll ignore you for an entire day. Give them cuddles, and they'll give you a scratch on your cheek that will leave you feeling insecure for weeks. For this reason, it's hard to know what the town of Gander was thinking when it tried to impose restrictions on local cats. Under the Municipalities Act of 1990, "if any cat shall cause damage to any lawn, grass plot, garden, or flower bed and flower, shrub or plant, such cat shall be deemed to be a nuisance and the owner thereof shall be deemed to have committed an offence in terms of these regulations." Don't eat plants or we'll fine your owners? That's the best lawmakers could offer? If Gander really wanted to motivate its feline residents to behave, they could have thrown in some added incentives: catnip, chin rubs, maybe some warm milk.

RUFFLING FEATHERS: Once upon a time, rural townships enjoyed the simple pleasure of being able to walk out into their backyard, collect some eggs from their personal chicken coops, and make omelets for the family. Now, such policies are being rolled back to accommodate the wants of quickly gentrifying neighborhoods who want to strip their rural reputations and reinvent themselves. Take the town of Conception Bay South. In 2016, a pair of cops showed up on the doorstep of Alicia Penney-Harnum, demanding that she remove a single hen from her backyard. In recent years, such laws have become more common, forcing many farmers to shift to the "go to the grocery store and buy a dozen eggs like everyone else" model.

IT'S HOT IN HERE: It doesn't matter how desperate you are for your morning cup of coffee. If there's a fire within two hundred meters of your local Dunkin' Donuts, you are out of luck; operating a vehicle near an active conflagration is not allowed in the town of Gander. Apparently it could "obstruct fire fighters" and stop them from "saving lives." How inconvenient.

NOVA SCOTIA

Whales as Far as the Eye Can See

NO SHOES, NO SHIRT, NO SERVICE: When passengers get into a cab, they agree to a few unspoken rules like "don't barf on the seats" and "don't cry so much that everyone else in the car becomes uncomfortable." But you know that drivers have rules they must abide by too? One rule commonly seen across Nova Scotia, Canada, restricts what drivers can and can't wear while on the job. This bylaw taken from the Yarmouth city ordinances, for example, states that "every driver, while in control of a taxi or accessible taxi, shall wear a shirt or military type blouse with a collar and sleeves (no T-shirts), ankle-length trousers or dress shorts which are worn within at least three inches of the knee, socks and shoes, which clothing shall be in a neat and tidy condition. Every driver may, in place of ankle-length trousers, wear a skirt." In short: no shorts, no T-shirts, or no service.

TOTALLY SPIES: FBI agents are going to have to find another place to stake out their suspects because in Halifax, Canada, spying on people in a public park is off-limits. As bylaw P-601 notes, "while in any park, no person shall . . . create a nuisance by spying, accosting, frightening, annoying or otherwise disturbing other persons." Logically, this makes sense: anyone looking for peace of mind through a quiet stroll in the park won't be able to find it if they spot a group of men in black watching their every move.

ONTARIO
Falling for Niagara

KEEP MY HORSE: Didn't pay your hotel bill? Don't think you can ride off into the sunset without any consequences. In Ontario, the Innkeepers Act says that "an innkeeper, livery-stable keeper or boarding-stable keeper who has a lien upon a horse, other animal or carriage for the value or price of any food or accommodation supplied, or for care or labor bestowed thereon, has, in addition to all other remedies provided by law, the right, in case the same remains unpaid for two weeks, to sell by public auction the horse." In other words, if you don't settle your hotel bill, the hotel owner can sell your horse. While this law may seem antiquated, it was actually passed in 1990, suggesting that penny-pinching horseback riders are very much still a problem.

HAMMER IT HOME: So, your IKEA bed frame delivery was delayed and showed up on your doorstep at 9:00 p.m. Time to hunker down and put it together, right? Not if you live in Red Lake, Canada. In this tiny town, hammering between the hours of 9:00 p.m. and 7:00 a.m. is illegal. In fact, "the operation of any tool including a hammer, saw, nail gun, lawn mower, staple gun, hedge trimmer, drill or the like, except for purposes of any snow removal" is illegal. How one could use a staple gun to remove snow is unclear, but Canadians are smart. They could probably find a way.

PRINCE EDWARD ISLAND

We Put the Anne in Green Gables

DING-DONG DITCH: There's an elementary school tradition where, around Halloween, children fill a bag with candy, place it on a friend's doorstep, ring the bell, and run away as fast as they can, leaving behind a set of instructions that encourage the receiver of the candy to "continue the chain" and deliver a new bag to another classmate. Called Being Booed, this activity is a creative way to celebrate the holiday and get a bag of goodies to stuff your face with. It's also an easy way to get arrested if you live in the town of Souris on Prince Edward Island. According to one bylaw, "any person who, willfully or wantonly, rings any doorbell or knocks at any door, building or fence ... so as to disturb or annoy any person in his/her dwelling, place of business, or meeting place is guilty of an offence." In short, no ding-dong ditching or you'll be spending Halloween in a jail cell.

TINY MEN: Scrap those plans to build a Godzilla out of snow. The town of Souris is not having it. According to a number of very passionate Canadians, it is illegal to build a snowman over thirty inches in this area. Now, that would be truly absurd . . . if it were true. We were unable to dig up a source confirming the existence of such a law, meaning your idea for a monster snowman is still on the table.

QUEBEC
Poutine on the Ritz

HEY, I WAS DRINKING THAT: The world is barreling toward a water crisis. With climate change on the rise and the planet's resources dwindling at an unprecedented rate, we are years away from seeing water companies on the stock market and Mad Max societies popping up in desert areas. Beaconsfield seems to have caught onto this trend early. This city in the province of Quebec prohibits anyone from wasting drinking water "to melt snow or ice on driveways, grounds, patios or sidewalks." Yes, drinking water melts snow pretty effectively, but you know what it can also do? Keep you alive.

UNLOCKED: Talk about a case of the Mondays. In 2019, a young woman named Lauren from Wakefield, Canada, trudged to her car to drive to work and kick off her long week, only to discover that she had received a parking ticket. More specifically, a 108-dollar parking ticket. Was it because she parked in a tow-away zone? Had she left her baby in the car? Was the vehicle covered in distracting bumper stickers like "Keep Quebec Weird" or "I'd Rather Be Fishing"? No. It was simply unlocked. According to one local bylaw, it is illegal to leave your car unlocked if it's parked on a public roadway. Apparently, you can be punished for feeling too safe in your community.

EXCUSE MY FRENCH: Not all Canadians appreciate the presence of "stupid Americans" on their land, as evidenced by this one Quebec law that requires the use of French (not English) on all public business signs. If the owner would like to include an English translation, they can, as long as the font used for the English text is at least two sizes smaller than the font used for the French inscriptions. Talk about petty.

JUST KEEP (NOT) SWIMMING: It's a blistering summer day and your mom tells you to run down to the local pool and "entertain yourself." What do you do? Trick question. If you're under eight years old and a resident of Montreal, you call the police, because swimming alone as a minor is illegal in this city. Prior to 2017, no such law existed to protect the rights of little swimmers, but after a few tragic pool-related incidents, the Quebec Lifesaving Society stepped in, working with the city on some new regulations to prevent any more deaths.

SASKATCHEWAN
Breadwinners

OH POO: Pick up after your pet. It's the first rule parents assign when they invest in a family dog, and one that one city in Saskatchewan, Canada, takes very seriously. In Tisdale, all dog owners are required to pick up their dog poop daily, or else be fined: "If a dog or other animal defecates on any public or private property . . . other than on the property of its owner, the owner of the animal shall cause the defecation to be removed immediately. Any person owning or occupying property in the Town of Tisdale shall remove any and all dog defecation from the said property on a daily basis and shall dispose of the defecation in a sanitary manner." It's a poopy situation, but one that everyone in Saskatchewan has to live with.

HOT AND BOTHERED: Imagine telling a pregnant woman that she can't leave the house. How would she react? Our guess is "not well." This is likely how female dogs feel about one ordinance in Estevan, Canada, that prevents canines in heat from going outside: "A female dog or cat in heat shall be confined and housed in the residence of the owner or person having control of the dog or cat or taken to a licensed kennel during the whole period that the dog or cat is in heat, except that a female dog or cat may be allowed outside the said residence for the sole purpose of permitting the dog or cat to defecate and urinate on the premises of the owner." While this law feels a bit restrictive to these animals, at the same time, it's hard to imagine a dog or cat on the verge of giving birth having the forethought to take a pee break before popping out a handful of full-grown babies.

NORTHWEST TERRITORIES
Mush Mush Mush

DOG EAT DOG: In Hay River, Canada, you cannot drive a dogsled on the sidewalk. There is some logic behind this oft quoted law, but it's a bit hard to follow so stick with me. There is a bylaw listed in the Municipal Corporation of the Town of Hay River in the Northwest Territories that outlines local rules for dog teams—groups of canines attached to sleds that drag their owners across great snowy expanses. Within this section, there is a provision that notes: "Unless otherwise posted, where a pathway or sidewalk passes through an area prohibited to dogs, dogs on a leash are permitted in such areas provided they remain on the defined pathway or sidewalk and are not running at large." The phrase "running at large" is key here because a group of huskies dashing through the snow could technically qualify as "running at large." Therefore, if dogsleds are considered "running at large" and "running at large" is not allowed on pathways, then, logically, dogsleds are not allowed on pathways. Make sense?

EGGS ON EGGS: The Wildlife Act for the Northwest Territories of Canada lays out some very important rules. Mainly, don't eat bird eggs. Well, unless you're starving and have no other choice. In that case, fry 'em up and swallow 'em down because under the emergencies and accidental kills subsection, "a person may harvest and consume wildlife or take and consume the eggs of birds if it is necessary to prevent starvation of a person." But for the record, before you go off and make a whole omelet out of some poor blue jay's babies, this passage also states that "you cannot use this section as an excuse to kill wildlife if the situation happened because of your own lack of planning or mismanagement." Nice try.

NUNAVUT
Igloos and Eskimos

CHEAPER THAN A TAXI: Something momentous happened in 2019 in the town of Iqaluit: cab fares went up one whole dollar, from a seven-dollar flat rate to an eight-dollar flat rate. For those of us who are accustomed to twenty-dollar Uber fares, a dollar might not seem like a lot, but in this 7,000-person town, that extra buck makes a difference. Nestled between the Labrador Sea and Hudson Bay at the tippity top of Canada, Iqaluit is a relatively remote town, boasting only twenty miles of land. With no Ubers or Lyfts in sight, residents must rely on taxi services to get around. That's why, in 2019, cab drivers—arguably, essential workers in Iqaluit—rallied together to increase their wages, arguing for a higher flat rate across the board. This is important to remember because the next time you try to hitch a ride into Iqaluit and the taxi driver demands anything more than eight dollars, you will know better than to fall for their tricks.

NO BEER HERE: For years, liquor stores were not allowed in the territory of Nunavut. Why? Because when you live in the middle of nowhere, and there's nothing else to do, people turn to the bottle, and the officials of Nunavut wanted to avoid the problems that accompany that decision. But over the years, the area has become more open to the idea of liquor stores, thanks to some very vocal citizens who were tired of driving ten-plus miles to get a bottle of wine. The territory has since launched a number of beer and wine stores in places like Iqaluit to test the waters and, while there's been some uptick in alcohol-related incidents, overall, the people of Nunavut seem to be handling their liquor well.

YUKON
Wild, Wild Wilderness

HIGHWAY TO HELL: There aren't many things more maddening than traffic. Humans weren't designed to sit in small, heated metal boxes with their children for five-plus hours. While we have found some ways to cope (podcasts, good music, long phone calls with family members you haven't talked to in years because, they're chatterboxes and, frankly, you just haven't had the time), these methods haven't entirely cured our frustrations and our desire to take them out on the highways that entrap us using a sledgehammer or whatever other sharp object we can find. Unfortunately for residents of Dawson City, Canada, that's not really an option. Per one Yukon-area bylaw, "no person shall . . . excavate or otherwise destruct a highway, including the road allowance thereof." Invest in a stress ball instead.

SMELLS LIKE DANGER: In Dawson City, you cannot transport any material that may imperil the lives of the area's residents. What exactly does that mean? Well, it could mean anything. Nuclear weapons? A truck of serial killers? A cage filled with very hungry chickens? All of these items would probably result in catastrophe and could be off-limits under this bylaw.

ACKNOWLEDGMENTS

It's hard to know who to acknowledge in a book about local laws. Do I thank Massachusetts, who provided just enough snow to keep me inside the house and focused, allowing me to finish these pages in time for Christmas? Do I thank the Midwest, for teaching me more about hunting laws than I ever cared to know? Or do I thank America in general for having the guts to flee the British all those years ago, so that decades later, I could plop down in front of my laptop and revel in the odd ordinances that each state has collected? I can't decide, so instead, I'll stick with the obvious acknowledgments. Thank you to John Whalen, my wonderful publisher at Whalen Book Works for giving me the opportunity to learn more about the world, my designer, Bryce de Flamand, for making this book look beautiful, and my editor, Margaret McGuire Novak, for patiently editing all of my bad jokes. Thank you to my illustrator June Lee, for penning the pictures that brought these words to life. Thank you to my family and friends, for enduring all of my "Did you know . . . " interjections for months. And most of all, thank you to this book, for being one of the only bright lights in the dark year that was 2020. So long, farewell, and good riddance.

ABOUT THE AUTHOR

Tyler Vendetti is a writer, reader, and all around "creative"—a grossly Hollywood term that she both loves and hates. She's the author of the Illustrated Compendium series, a set of gift books dedicated to the weirdest, ugliest, and most hip words in the English language. Your aunt has probably read one. When she's not researching language or obscure state ordinances, Tyler works in the entertainment industry, doing everything from reading scripts to fetching coffee to quietly panicking over celebrity interactions. She lives in Los Angeles like everyone else in the biz and can be found on Twitter @HeyThereFuture or in her apartment paying far too much in rent.

ABOUT THE ILLUSTRATOR

June Lee is a graphic designer and illustrator who enjoys everything communication design–related, from painting murals to branding design. Projects include the Truth Campaign for *The New York Times*, Pizzaz Pizza Festival, and *Junk* magazine. In her free time, June can be found reading with a cup of coffee in hand, or out hunting for the best coffee in the city. She lives in Brooklyn, New York. For more of her work, visit juneleedesign.com.

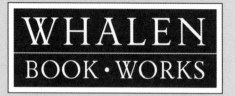

PUBLISHING PRACTICAL & CREATIVE NONFICTION

Whalen Book Works is a small, independent book publishing company based in Kennebunkport, Maine, that combines top-notch design, unique formats, and fresh content to create truly innovative gift books.

Our unconventional approach to bookmaking is a close-knit, creative, and collaborative process among authors, artists, designers, editors, and booksellers. We publish a small, carefully curated list each season, and we take the time to make each book exactly what it needs to be.

We believe in giving back. That's why we plant one tree for every ten books we sell. Your purchase supports a tree in the Rocky Mountain National Park. 🌲

Get in touch!

Visit us at Whalenbooks.com or write to us at
68 North Street, Kennebunkport, ME 04046.

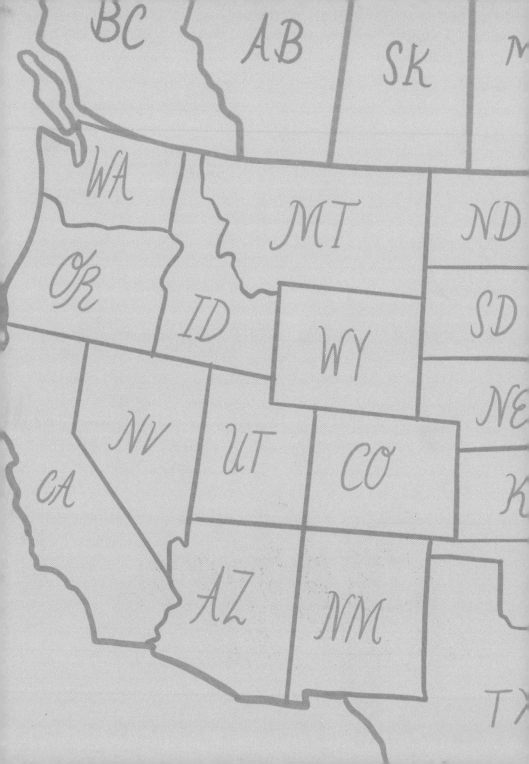